PLAY THUNO

The World-Changing Multiplication Game

GOD'S CALL AND POWER TO BECOME A LEVEL 5IVE CHURCH

BY LARRY WALKEMEYER

EXPONENTIAL

WITH THANKS TO...

Exponential

Thank you Todd Wilson, Bill Cochenour, Terri Saliba, Lindy Lowry (especially you, the tireless whiz of editing), Karen Pheasant, Eric Reiss and the rest of the exceptional Exponential team for your unflagging labor to multiply the message of church multiplication. Your genuine selflessness is a powerful role model to church leaders everywhere. You exemplify the posture essential for multiplication—humility, faith, hard work, love and courage. I am honored to be part of such a family. May many churches "Become 5" because of you.

Light & Life Christian Fellowship

You are my teammates in this adventure of learning to *play thuno*. You are refusing the comfort of "addition" for the power of "multiplication." Your faith and sacrifice have already launched multiple leaders and churches locally and internationally; yet you are willing to courageously move forward towards being a "Level 5" church, a multiplication movement. Your love and support for my Kingdom work far beyond our local body are received as a grace from God through you. Thank you. I love you church!

Azusa Pacific University

As a new member of the APU Board of Trustees, I am privileged to begin employing the terminology of "our" when I refer to APU. Our motto of "God First" is woven into the fabric of our organization at every level. Our passion is to play our part in seeing "God's Kingdom come" in every sphere of society, particularly the local church. Thank you for allowing my work to be part of this effort. May our tribe multiply.

Free Methodist Church in Southern California

There are many good denominations and tribes expanding God's Kingdom. I am blessed to be part of one of the great ones. Multiplication is a team "sport" done better together than alone. Thank you for your love, prayers, wisdom, friendship and financial support. They have empowered me to *play thuno* (multiply) in our city, our Southern California region and remote unreached international areas.

And Finally...

High fives and huge hugs to *mi familia*!

Kids—Anjelica, TJ and Linz—my superlative times in life are skiing down picturesque mountain slopes with you or listening to you pray around our dinner table. Your love and laughter ennoble my life far more than any applause or position. Proud to be your dad.

Deb—my dear Dr. Deb. My love for you grows with every turn of the calendar page. Your wisdom enriches me. Your prayers empower me. Your compassion enthralls me. My best "thank you" is but a morsel of the feast of gratitude you truly deserve.

INSIDE

FOREWORD

It would be difficult for me to more enthusiastically endorse a new book. Simply stated, Larry Walkemeyer has written the book I wish I'd written. So I rejoice that this important book is completed at the work of a good friend's hand.

I first met Larry when Exponential announced we would be taking our annual conference to the West Coast. He was an immediate advocate for us and quickly became a friend of Exponential. Anyone who has met and spent any time with Larry knows that this guy bleeds church multiplication. I'm thankful that he has allowed God to work and speak through him as a role model for living out multiplication in his life and the church he leads. I appreciate him using his passion to write about the biblical call to multiply the Church.

That same passion drives Exponential. The goal of seeing the Church multiply led Dave Ferguson and I to write the book *Becoming a Level 5 Multiplying Church Field Guide*. We wanted to identify the characteristics of five levels of church multiplication and introduce a new vocabulary for church leaders. Ultimately, we dream about seeing the needle on U.S. church multiplication move from less than four percent of churches reproducing to greater than 10 percent. I know Larry has the same dream.

This book you're about to read serves as an excellent follow-up resource to *Becoming 5*. *Play Thuno* shares inspiring stories and practical examples of multiplication that the Church needs to discover and highlight. To become Level 5 multiplying churches, we need models to give us tangible expressions of what it looks like to take to heart the biblical call to multiply. Larry tells the multiplication story of the church he's leading, Light & Life Christian Fellowship in Long Beach, California, and also shares stories of other churches that are multiplying, carrying the fullness of Jesus into their communities and cities.

Thankfully, he is candid in his storytelling, sharing the tensions and even failures Light & Life has encountered in their zeal to multiply. In his transparency, we see ourselves. In his honesty, we see our churches. Larry shows us that while the road to multiplication is far from smooth, it is still doable because Scripture has intentionally and clearly called us to follow this path. He presses into the reality that while every church has Level 5 multiplication potential, they almost always settle for Level 3 addition because they simply don't know *how* to move into multiplication.

To that end, *Play Thuno* also offers practical and clear thinking needed in the pursuit of Level 5 multiplication. Each chapter delivers specific insights for igniting multiplication in your church, including urgent reasons to multiply, traits of biblical multiplication, a close look at the deceptions that derail multiplication and even 21 essentials for leading a church of multipliers.

One note: You may think you've heard everything there is to hear about the Acts church and might be tempted to skip over or skim Larry's exploration. I urge you not to. The insights Larry offers through the lens of multiplication are fresh and vital to seeing and embracing God's plan for His Church, and ultimately the world. His unique study of the early Church is deserving of your time and attention.

Larry wrote this book to motivate the American Church towards becoming a Level 5 church. I'm thankful for leaders like him who are so bent on seeing the Church multiply that they're compelling their churches and other leaders to ask, "What would it look like for our church to multiply? How would it change our community? How would it change our world?"

I pray that *Play Thuno* compels you and your church to ask those questions and become a Level 5 multiplying church that risks to reach our world.

—Todd Wilson, founder and director of Exponential,
and author of *More: Find Your Personal Calling and
Live Life to the Fullest Measure*

INTRODUCTION

Discovering the Game

In author Suzanne Collins' wildly best-selling trilogy, *The Hunger Games*, we read about a society shaped by the game it's forced to play—a game of death. In a far more widely circulated book, we find an invitation to a different kind of "game"—a game of life.

Introduced in the Bible's first chapter, this game of life remains ever-present throughout Scripture's 1,189 chapters. When this game is played, it reproduces life—sown into the fabric of all of God's creation. As humans, we were created and divinely designed to play this game. God's first command to the first humans He created was to engage in the game of life. Woven into our physiques are the essentials we need to engage in it.

Recently, while researching the topic of multiplication in Scripture, I had one of those "aha" moments. Acts 9:31 ends this way: "*...and the church multiplied.*" In this context, the Greek word for multiplied is *plēthynō*. Not being a Greek scholar, I hit the pronunciation button and heard a deep, sonorous voice that basically sounded like, "play thuno." As I searched out other verses for *plēthynō* references in the Septuagint, I discovered it again in Genesis 1:28:

> "*God blessed them; and God said to them, 'Be fruitful and multiply, and fill the earth, and subdue it ... '*"

I still remember the goose bumps I felt as I distinctly heard God calling me into the game/work/mission of church "multiplication."

Now I realize that this scripture refers to God's admonition to Adam and Eve to physically reproduce. Let's be honest, this scripture has been one of my favorite "go to" verses in my marriage. However, I believe a treasure trove of theology, missiology and ecclesiology also is ensconced in this short directive. God was also speaking of the mission of His bride.

Genesis 1:26-28 powerfully frames His intention, action and invitation:

- The "Great Consultation" among the Godhead (Gen. 1:26): *"Let us make mankind in our image, in our likeness, so that they may rule..."* is followed by...
- The "Great Creation" by the Godhead (Gen.1:27): *"So God created mankind in his own image, in the image of God he created them; male and female he created them"* is followed by...
- The "Great Commission" from the Godhead (Gen. 1:28): *"God blessed them; and God said to them, "Be fruitful and multiply, and fill the earth, and subdue it."*

Understanding these three premises gives me exceptional confidence to engage in this multiplication game. Realizing...

1. We are designed by God's forethought as a reflection of His creative, life-giving character.
2. We are produced by and endowed with the DNA, as it were, of God Himself. We bear in our bodies the same multiplicative capacity we see Him exercise in creation.
3. We are commanded to fully participate and co-labor with God in the "game" of multiplication.

A Silent Disease

When I was a sixth grader, I decided one night to start reading the Bible. I hauled our big King James off the coffee table and into my bedroom. I naively thought the best place to start was the beginning of the book. I was only a couple of minutes in when I arrived at the creation of humans and the first words God said to them in, you guessed it, Genesis 1:28: *"... Be fruitful, and multiply, and replenish the earth, and subdue it ... ."*

I had little idea what words like "fruitful," "replenish," or "subdue," meant, but as a Kansas farm boy who raised rabbits, I was very clear about the word "multiply." I was old enough to understand the birds and the bees partly because I had watched my rabbits.

If there is one mission that rabbits are good at, it is breeding and multiplying. God designed rabbits to be multiplication machines. They reach sexual maturity at six months, their gestation period is just 30 days, and the day after they give birth, they can get pregnant again. In an average lifespan of 10 years, one rabbit can "multiply" 1,000 times.

As a sixth-grade boy, I was counting the fortune my rabbits would bring me. But just as my rabbit fortunes began to build, a disease swept through the rabbit pens. My rabbits were no longer interested in multiplying. Instead, their energy was given to survival. Many of them died before the medicine could take effect.

As I flash back on my rabbit-raising days, I glimpse a picture of the Church of Jesus in America. A silent disease has infiltrated our ranks subverting our natural desire for multiplication. We have forgotten our original DNA. Our image-bearing reality of being co-creators with God has been buried beneath the cultural baggage of what it means to be the church in an age of entertainment and consumerism.

For the most part, we have disengaged from *play thuno*.

Becoming Five

In their watershed book, *Becoming a Level 5 Multiplying Church*, authors Todd Wilson and Dave Ferguson describe five levels of churches in America today:

- Level 1 is a church in decline: a "subtracting" church.
- Level 2 is a plateaued church: a "surviving" church.
- Level 3 is a growing church: an "adding" church.
- Level 4 is a church that plants another church: a "reproducing" church.
- Level 5 is a church built around multiplication: a "multiplying" church.[1]

Using those classifications and based on research, the church in America reveals a troubling picture. Some 80 percent of churches in America are at Levels 1 and 2. Less than four percent are at Level 4, and less than .005 percent of churches in America are at Level 5. We have a multiplication problem; the rabbits are sick.

I wrote this book in an effort to motivate the Church, especially the American Church, towards becoming a Level 5 church—the natural convergence of Jesus and His Church. God's command to Adam and Eve was for their relationship to bring forth multiplication of life. Scripture identifies Adam as symbolic of Christ and Eve as symbolic of the Church. When this relationship is healthy and intimate, offspring is expected. Their offspring would possess a certain distinct capability—the ability to reproduce.

The goal was not for Adam and Eve to have a big family. Perhaps they did. We know of Cain, Abel and Seth, but Scripture also tells us they had "other sons and daughters" (Gen. 5:4). The call was something different than *adding* children to the family. The call was to "multiply," to produce children who had the desire and capacity to produce other children. No matter how many children Adam and Eve had, they could never fulfill God's call unless they moved from addition to multiplication. They couldn't "fill the earth and reign over it" unless they reproduced children who would reproduce.

That's why I join almost all other Bible translations in taking exception to the NIV's translation of Genesis 1:28: "... Be fruitful and increase in number...." Because the word *plēthynō* is defined "to increase, to multiply," it can and should be translated as "increase"—at times. However, if we use the word "increase" in Genesis 1:28, we miss something of significance—the call to multiply, the invitation to *play thuno*!

This book is designed to motivate you to get in the game, or if you're already in the game, to be a higher impact player. I share biblical rationale, illustrations, true stories and key principles designed to impassion our hearts, overhaul our thinking, and engage us in action.

I believe every church was birthed with the capacity and calling to multiply. The game of *play thuno* is not for an elite class of churches. Most importantly, it is for *your* church.

1

Playing the Game

5 Urgent Reasons to Multiply

"Why don't you come over tonight and play Settlers of Catan?"

I had no clue what this young pastor was talking about, so I asked him to explain the game he was talking about. After a brief description that left me with more questions than answers, I said to him, "Just tell me *why* I should come play."

He immediately answered, "Because it's the best game in the world and you get to hang out with me!"

Play thuno is the best game in the world, and you get to hang out with people who love Jesus! But there are other important factors in *why* you should engage wholeheartedly in multiplication. Let me offer the five most urgent reasons you'll love this game—five motivations to reach for Level 5 multiplication.

Reason #1 To improve the health of the Church

If you love the Church of Jesus, you will love this game.

Often church planting or multiplication is seen as a threat to the current and future health of the parent or "sending" church. Certainly, this is a possibility—if we plant without prayer and planning, or out of the wrong motivation. But aside from blatant missteps like these, multiplication can be one of the best tonics for the health of your church.

Recent evidence bears that out. In a 2014 *Christianity Today* article, LifeWay Research President Ed Stetzer talked about a study of 75 churches of different sizes that were all planting churches. The study compared those churches with 75 churches that were not planting and found that the planting churches were actually healthier than the non-planting churches.[1]

This study and other research indicate that one of the best ways to improve the health of your church is to plant another church. Planting drives the Church back to the vitality of its original mission. While it may seem counter-intuitive by today's standards of success, we're talking about Kingdom logic. By sacrificially giving, we receive more of God's blessing. That goes for us individually, as well as for churches. There is no better way to give than to daughter a new church from your existing church.

The concept of "sending" not only fosters healthiness in the mother church, it also imparts a vital DNA into the churches that are birthed. Instead of the typical "us-centeredness" and "addiction to addition" conditions that can be so prevalent in church plants, new churches birthed out of multiplication start with a culture of vivacity and generosity that flows from a selfless, multiplication orientation. With that DNA, the Kingdom possibilities are endless. A church with this kind of culture is poised to multiply, possibly a new chain of multiplying churches.

Reason #2 To reach unique groups of people

If you love all types of people, you will love this game.

I have an unchurched friend who would never step foot in a megachurch, while another tells me the only church he would ever considering visiting is a megachurch. I like to believe my biker friend, cowboy friend, rocker friend and college professor friend would all attend the same church … and they might, eventually. At first, however, each will be most likely to attend a church that has some of his or her personal "vibe."

In the article I mentioned above, Stetzer reminds us, "People think America is a pancake, uniformly flat—people thinking and living the same. America is not a pancake; it is a waffle. A waffle with thousands of little divots with people of different cultures, customs and contexts." [2] A plethora of new churches in all kinds of places, in every nook and cranny, led by a vast variety of leaders will reach the greatest harvest in America.

Reason #3 To follow the biblical pattern

If you love the Bible, you will love this game.

The multiplication concept of *play thuno* fills the pages of the New Testament. In the early Church, planting new churches that trained and released other church planters was the simple method that allowed the gospel to take root in the first century. The seeds of the gospel did not just land and spring up for a moment; they put down foundational roots, allowing the plants to grow and reproduce other seed.

If you've ever blown vigorously on a mature dandelion, you've seen the seeds take flight and scatter into new territory. But if you followed those seeds, you'd inevitably discover that some didn't take root. Instead of producing a new generation of dandelions, these seeds were easily whisked away by the wind.

Church planters in the New Testament didn't just take the gospel message to others; they took the social structure of the Church. This organization, however informal in structure, gave the gospel a holding place where the roots could go down deep, grow up, and then reproduce.

The biblical pattern from Genesis 1 shows us that healthy organisms reproduce after their own kind. Every healthy church should grow into a reproducing mother. This is a sign of maturity, regardless of the church's size. It is the multi-generational legacy God desires for every church.

Reason #4 To honor Jesus with obedience

If you love Jesus and desire to follow His directive, you will love this game.

Jesus was clear in word and deed, instruction and example, message and model: *God's method for carrying out the mission is multiplication.* Jesus was confident of changing the world, not just because of His message, or His divine power, but because of the method He was using to reach the world.

While the other "pseudo-messiahs" of His era sought to collect crowds and mount a rebellion, Jesus spent His time pouring the purity of His DNA into a handful of ordinary, unschooled disciples—keeping His original promise to them. In Matthew 4:19, He invites them to, "Come, follow me, and I will send you out to fish for people." "Following" Jesus didn't mean going where He went, but rather taking His yoke—His unique teaching and method of ministry—and emulating it.

The disciples spent approximately three years "learning of Him" (Matt. 11:29), and at the end of His time on earth, He gave them their marching orders: *"Therefore go and make disciples of all nations, baptizing them in the name of the Father and of the Son and of the Holy Spirit"* (Matt. 28:19), essentially, "Go fish for people … go reproduce yourself … go make some disciples who will keep this chain reaction moving."

It wasn't cool, hip or flashy. It was personal. It was work. It was real. It was obedience: "Make a disciple who will make a disciple." Jesus understood that a handful of multiplying disciples is bigger than any crowd would ever be.

Yet this Jesus model is almost entirely ignored in our churches today. In my work, I visit different churches from various backgrounds, and it never fails. If I ask, "How many of your members are actively making disciples who make disciples?" immediately the pastor begins to uncomfortably squirm. Regardless of church size, I've never had a pastor give me a number higher than 1 percent of their members. As Exponential has discovered, churches that are discipling the Jesus way and giving birth to churches that also actively reproduce (Level 5 churches) are almost non-existent in the American church.

We don't choose multiplication because it's a fad, or even because it works. We certainly don't choose it because it's fast or easy. We choose it because Jesus is Lord, and He commands His subjects, "Go make disciples … ." Our obedience is an act of worship that glorifies Him and brings His goodness to us.

Reason #5 - To reach the most lost people
If you love those without Christ, you will love this game!

There is simply no comparison between addition and multiplication. Consider… If you took a simple checkerboard or chessboard and placed a single sugar cube on each square, you would end up with 64 sugar cubes. That is addition.

If, on the other hand, you simply multiplied by two the number of sugar cubes you put on each square … for example put one cube on square #1, and then doubled that for square #2, and then doubled that for square

#3, and continued to double until you reached square #64, you would have enough sugar to cover the state of Texas with 30 feet of sugar.

Such is the power of multiplication.

Imagine the person you lead to Christ or who responds to your message with a decision for Christ as the one sugar cube you place on the square next to you. If you don't teach him to reproduce himself, you simply add one "cube" to the Kingdom—noble, but not powerful work. You'll spend your life filling up the board God gave you. But so much more is possible. Through multiplication, you could cover Texas!

The same is true for churches. Most never even add one more church in the square next to them. Instead, they build a big tower in the square they're in (Level 3 "Adding" church), but never fill another square (Level 4 "Reproducing" church), let alone begin to multiply (Level 5 "Multiplying" church).

You may have heard the phrase "God has a mission; therefore there is a church." Jesus came on a mission to "seek and to save the lost" (Luke 19:10). To carry out His mission, He laid down His life on the cross. Salvation was accomplished, but the mission was not finished.

As eternity-altering as the cross is, more than atonement happened at Calvary. At the cross, the Church was born. The Church was inaugurated to carry out Christ's mission to the world. Each time a gospel-bearing church is planted, a fresh outpost for the mission is built. I imagine a vast city spreading out for miles. Each Jesus-exalting church is a bell tower, ringing the freedom bell. The attractive sound of its call rings out all over the neighborhood. But travel just a few streets over, and you can no longer hear its loving, urgent call. How do we address this reality?

The answer is not in higher bell towers or bigger bells.

Studies show us that new churches have three to four times the conversion rate per attendee than established churches do.4 Not only is multiplication more proficient, it also is more prolific—starting new points of mission in more diverse places. New churches are more likely to plant new churches that, in turn, will reach the lost.[3]

If we're genuinely urgent about rescuing lost people, we will prioritize planting. Observant church researchers agree that the most effective way to carry out the mission of the church is not to add, but to multiply.

We need *more* bell towers. God desires that one be in every neighborhood until wherever you journey, you hear the gentle, beautiful song of the bells calling you to the freedom found in Christ.

2

The Priority of the Game

4 Phases of Gospel Multiplication

G od invites all people to get out of the grandstands and onto the game field and *play thuno*. His expansion plan for His people has always been accomplished through multiplication. As you journey from Genesis through the gospels, you find this emphasis on the DNA of multiplication. A quick survey of a few people and places in Scripture reveals the priority of the game.

Adam

As we've already said, "multiply" was the first command to Adam and Eve. They had no sex manual. God may have said, "Come together, be unified in My love, in obedience to Me, in faith that a miracle of reproduction can happen. Then be patient, and an astounding event will occur. There will be new little 'images of God' running around, spreading My rule and reign over My creation. And they, too, will have the capacity to multiply."

Noah

Play thuno was again the command when God flooded the earth and repopulated it. Restoration offered the potential for a new beginning, for the people God created to know Him, to love Him, and to promote His glory to the rest of creation. Thus, God gave Noah the same command as Adam, "Be fruitful and multiply."

Abraham

Play thuno was God's promise to Abraham—and to the world. Multiplication would be the means by which the world would receive blessing and hope. As Abraham's seed multiplied, a people who lived by faith in the one true God would expand throughout the earth inviting others to join them as the "people of God."

Babylonian captivity

Play thuno was still God's strategy when His people were captives in a foreign land, ripped out of their home country and living in the oppressive strangeness of Babylon. God tells His people, *"Take wives and become the fathers of sons and daughters, and take wives for your sons and give your daughters to husbands, that they may bear sons and daughters; and multiply there and do not decrease"* (Jer. 29:6, NASB). It is as if God says, "You can multiply even when it's difficult and if you don't, you will decrease."

Post-Babylonian captivity

Multiplication was God's future hope-filled promise to His exiled people while they were in Babylon. Not only were they to multiply while in Babylon, His promise was multiplication upon their return: "Then I Myself will gather the remnant of My flock out of all the countries where I have driven them and bring them back to their pasture, and they will be fruitful and multiply" (Jer, 23:3, NASB). They had the promise of multiplication to look forward to.

Jesus

When the fullness of time came, God planted a seed in a virgin (Gen. 3:17, Gal. 4:4). The nature of a seed is that it will be planted in the ground, die, spring back to life and reproduce multiples of its own kind. This is the Jesus story. He Himself would be the seed that died only to rise to new life, which would be multiplied into millions of disciples.

The Disciples

Multiplication began even before the resurrection and Pentecost. When Jesus matured, He immediately began to multiply. As He launched His ministry, He called 12 followers, a dozen apprentices.

His call to them is not complex. It stretches in two directions:

- "Follow me. Watch what I do and how I do it and even more importantly observe *why* I do it. Yes, learn My habits but above all gain My heart."
- "Go and *be Me* to the world. If you gain My heart, you will live on My mission. I will be multiplied through you. You will be Christians, 'little Christs,' spreading My teaching, compassion and power to the world around you." In essence, Jesus told His disciples, "If you watch Me, you will learn to *play thuno*."

If we want to learn to multiply, we must live in this synergy of "following" *and* "fishing"; "coming to Him" *and* "going for Him"; and "gaining His heart" *and* "giving His heart." This bi-directional call must frame our daily living.

After launching His ministry, Jesus very quickly demonstrates His priority on multiplication, calling ordinary men to the extraordinary mission of making disciples that make disciples.

Four Phases of Multiplication

The gospel of Mark highlights the approach that Jesus took to transform His disciples from followers to multipliers. From chapter 3 to chapter 6, Jesus moved the 12 through four phases—from (1) invitation to (2) education to (3) observation and finally to (4) participation in multiplication.

Phase 1 The Invitation to Multiplication (Mark 3)

Mark 3:13-15 tells us, *"Jesus went up on a mountainside and called to him those he wanted, and they came to him. He appointed twelve that they might be with him and that he might send them out to preach and to have authority to drive out demons."*

So Jesus called, and His chosen ones came to Him. Once they were there, He officially identified them as the 12 witnesses or messengers of His mission: "You are My 'A' team in this 'game.'" But we usually read past the power of the next phrase in verse 14: "… that they might be *with him.*" Companionship, friendship, doing life together, and walking with Him and each other would form the basis of this preparation for multiplication. By doing life with Him, the disciples would follow Jesus into His mission.

However, not long after He says, "I want you with Me," He tells them, "I want to send you out." Jesus says, "You are not *with me* just so we can go on nature hikes and barbecue lake trout together. You are *with me* so you can learn the game … so you can multiply and fill the earth. You will be living in this bi-vocational life of "being with Me" and "going for Me."

Motivation often flows from imitation. Ever gotten close to someone who's on fire for something, and you suddenly start to feel stirred over the same thing? I remember when I started hanging out with Christian leaders who were passionate about church planting. I had never thought much about how new churches were born. I guess I thought the denominational stork just dropped them off. But as I continued to talk with church planters, I began to catch their fire. I wanted to emulate them.

The models and leaders we admire will usually be what we end up reproducing. One of the most helpful things potential church planters can do is to spend quality time with those who are launching churches. Church planters and movement makers, make it a practice to invite potential planters to come alongside you and learn.

Phase 2 The Education of Multiplication (Mark 4)

Mark 4 starts with Jesus teaching His friends about the power of *play thuno*. Jesus tells the parable of the soil, the seed and the sower. The punchline is Mark 4:8: *"Still other seed fell on good soil. It came up, grew and produced a crop, some multiplying thirty, some sixty, some a hundred times."*

Jesus drives home the truth that the power of multiplication is in our hands.

He calls them to take the seed He has given them—the Word of God— and plant it into their personal fields, and then watch that seed multiply 30, 60, 100 times. But the seed is not only the Word of God; it's the disciples themselves. Jesus will eventually plant His disciples in the field to create this harvest of multiplication. This message is so vital that Jesus ends His parable by saying, "Whoever has ears to hear, let them hear" (Mark 4:9).

As church leaders, we must be fully convinced of the beauty and power of multiplication. The motivation that carries us through the disappointments of hard, shallow and rocky soils must be the conviction that "seed in good soil multiplies." That truth can far out produce the setbacks of the other three soils. We must passionately believe that multiplying disciples and churches is the most effective way to reach the most lost people for Christ.

It's true that as individual disciples we reach people through addition, adding one person at a time. But when we reach someone, do we have "addition" or "multiplication" in view? Do we reach him as a "convert" or as a "disciple" who's ready to move forward with the Commission? Do we claim victory when she signs on the dotted line for her ticket to Heaven or when she signs the covenant to make disciples? The first scenario is addition; the second is multiplication.

I think of two different "Scott's" I have led to Christ. The first Scott was a carnal, skirt-chasing cool guy who had a crisis and was open to the gospel. I celebrated his conversion, notched my gospel belt and hoped for the best for the rest of his life. His life has had no discernible impact for the Kingdom. The second Scott was a teen in my youth group who came to Christ. After educating him on multiplication, I invested my life in Scott's, and today this disciple is a church leader impacting many with the gospel. A multiplication mindset takes the long-term view that a disciple is worth the effort.

The apple/orchard analogy captures the priority and passion for becoming a Level 5 multiplying church. We can count the number of seeds in one apple, but we cannot count the number of apples in one seed. Over time, one seed can multiply into a myriad of orchards.

Phase 3 The Observation of Multiplication (Mark 5)

In the next chapter of Mark's gospel, the disciples learn they won't just be sitting on hillsides hearing chalk talks about *play thuno*. They will be turning their learning into living, their theology into biography. In Mark

5, everything is about to get really real. Jesus will be taking them with Him into the adventure of on-the-job training.

Sure enough, as Mark 5 begins, all hell breaks loose … literally. Mark 5 chronicles the disciples' "being with Jesus" as the demoniac comes charging out of the graveyard. A legion of demons comes out of him, and possessed pigs go plunging into the sea. The disciples hear Jesus say to the liberated grave-dweller, "Go home to your own people (your field) and tell them how much the Lord has done for you … ." The disciples have just watched *play thuno* in action.

Mark 5 continues with Lazarus' resurrection, a miracle healing of a councilman's son and a powerful statement, which would become a mantra for the disciples to hang on to: "Don't be afraid, just believe" (Mark 5:36). The disciples watch, as this river of life flows from their leader into the lives of the people around them.

As the disciples observe from their front-row seats, they now see their hillside lessons turned into living color, flesh and blood, demons and spiritual power. This movement from invitation, to education, to observation begins to transform them into carriers of this multiplication DNA. Every multiplying church in America needs a robust internship program. Internships are not the exclusive territory of big churches with brilliant pastors. They are effective in any church that's daring to plant.

Admittedly, this is one of my failures. A haphazard approach to bringing potential church planters to the front row to watch our church in action has hurt our multiplication efforts. Through internships or their equivalent, eager students can touch, taste and see the multiplication energy flowing through the veins of the church. If I revise this book in five years, hopefully I'll be able to modify this paragraph significantly.

Phase 4 Participation in Multiplication (Mark 6)

The typical rabbinical training of Jesus' day lasted several years. My guess is the disciples thought their training would be similar. However, in just a brief period of time, perhaps a few months, the disciples go from commercial fishermen and IRS agents to amateur players in the game of *play thuno*.

In Mark 6, after a quick visit to his faithless hometown, Jesus makes a surprise announcement to His team: "It's time to play ball on your own. Time to take to the field without Me being physically present. Time to be sent, to multiply."

But why send them out now? After all, Jesus had been on the move doing much ministry with significant results. The crowd was expanding. Addition was happening. Look at Mark 6:6b: *"...Then Jesus went around teaching from village to village."* Jesus could have stuck with the addition game, but He suddenly pulls a game changer. It is as if He says, "Addition is not the most effective means by which My father's Kingdom increases. We must multiply!"

So Jesus calls the 12 to Himself and begins to send them out two by two, telling them that He has given them authority over impure spirits (Mark 6:7). Off went the amateurs, filled with fears but moved by faith. Mark tells us, *"they went out and preached that people should repent. They drove out many demons and anointed many sick people with oil and healed them"* (Mark 6:12-13).

It's interesting that in the next verse, Mark gives us some idea of the mission's effectiveness. Mark reports, *"King Herod heard about this, for Jesus' name had become well known."* Jesus had been drawing the crowds by addition, but once He changed the game to multiplication, His message began to go viral and shake up the enemy's kingdom.

Edgar Dale and subsequently many other researchers have asked, "What methods of teaching lead to the highest knowledge retention rates?" Their results: 5% for lecture, 10% for reading, 30% for demonstration, 50% for discussion group, 75% for practice by doing and 90% for teaching others.[1]

Could too much time in the classroom and not enough time in the field have led to deformed disciples who could theologize but struggle with Kingdom math—both addition and multiplication? Jesus' method was invitation, education, observation and participation followed by debrief—all in a concentrated time frame. As the disciples practiced what they had observed when they lived life with Jesus, their effectiveness increased exponentially.

Much of the cultural baggage attached to our church in America has slowed down our traveling speed. When all of the expectations of buildings, budgets, billboards, bands, bulletins, and baby-changing tables get added to the wagon of church planting, it's easy to see why so few disciples try, and even fewer church plants succeed. Our normative image of church may have to change before we see an exceptional multiplication movement.

These four phases of the multiplication process we see in Mark are still effective today, but they are somewhat like Lazarus. These phases need to be resurrected and set free from the cultural wrappings that are holding the living church captive.

The Expansion of Multiplication

In his gospel, Luke notes that Jesus did not teach only the 12 apostles to *play thuno*; He taught many others as well. Luke 10:1 records that Jesus also sent out 36 pairs of disciples—72 individuals who were in the process of becoming disciples.

These 72 again demonstrate Jesus' emphasis on multiplication. He didn't seek to gather people to increase the size of His congregation at Capernaum. Instead, Jesus was "going" and "sending" His followers to where the people were to multiply the points where the gospel could penetrate the culture.

What I find fascinating is the prayer that Jesus asked these 72 disciples to pray as they went from place to place. He told them, *"The harvest is plentiful, but the workers are few. Ask the Lord of the harvest, therefore, to send out workers into his harvest field"* (Luke 10:2). It seems Jesus was directing, "As you go as one multiplied from Me, pray consistently that God would raise up others as a multiplication of yourselves. As you are being sent, pray for others you can send, workers who will extend the work of the harvest in these ripe fields."

In completing our journey from Genesis through the gospels, we must end on a hilltop in Galilee. In Matthew 28, Jesus gathered His followers around Himself for a parting directive. It was like His last locker room talk to lay out the game plan that would lead to victory. His words carried authority, wisdom and fire! I challenge you to read them aloud right now with passion, like you're reading them for the first time:

> *"Then Jesus came to them and said, 'All authority in heaven and on earth has been given to me. Therefore go and make disciples of all nations, baptizing them in the name of the Father and of the Son and of the Holy Spirit, and teaching them to obey everything I have commanded you. And surely I am with you always, to the very end of the age"* (Matt. 28:18-20).

Did you hear Him? He tells us who He is, what we're to trade our lives for, and how that will happen. Jesus is the one with all authority, power and ability. You are the one who is to go. Jesus, the one with the power, will go with you, always, every time!

Don't miss the multiplication here. There is a specific way to "go"—by making disciples. If you go by making converts but not disciples, your life will have only the limited impact of addition. You will only reach the people you can physically touch. However, understanding the Jesus method of multiplication helps you expand your reach exponentially. If you "disciple" people to the point they actually make other disciples, then you reach those you would otherwise never touch.

In another post-resurrection appearance from Jesus, we hear this same message stated in a different way. On the first Easter evening, the disciples are trembling behind bolted doors fearing the Jewish leaders will find and crucify them also. Unexpectedly, Jesus is standing in their midst.

John records Jesus' first appearance to the disciples. Notice His first words after He has had to repeat, "Peace be with you," a couple of times to settle their thumping hearts. Jesus says, *"As the Father has sent me, I am sending you. And with that he breathed on them and said, 'Receive the Holy Spirit'"* (John 20:21-22). Jesus declares their multiplication commission: "You are sent ones who are to be senders of others the same way I have sent you." With this commission comes the same power and authority Matthew 28:18-20 offers us for carrying out the mission. Here, with a unique symbolic act Jesus breathes on them and imparts His presence (power and authority) through the indwelling Holy Spirit.

The Power of Level 5

From Adam through Jesus, we observe this demonstration of multiplication and a priority on filling the earth with the people of God through reproduction. Addition is never the strategy God uses to populate the world with His followers. Multiplication is the tactical pattern the Spirit flows through to reach the lost. Level 5 churches alone have the capacity to reach the burgeoning population of our lost world.

In their book, *Implementation Guide to Natural Church Development*, Christian Schwarz and Christopher Schalk offer the following example illustrating the power of multiplication: "Imagine a water lily growing on a pond with a surface of 14,000 square feet," they write. "The leaf of this species of water lily has a surface of 15.5 square inches. At the beginning of the year, the water lily has exactly one leaf. After one week, there are two leaves. A week later, four. After 16 weeks, half of the water surface is covered with leaves." The authors then ask *how long it will take until the second half of the pond is also covered?* Another 16 weeks? No. It will take just a single week, and the pond will be completely covered.[2]

I can imagine the Roman Empire laughing at the small band of ordinary folks following a crucified messiah. Their talk of changing the world must have been a party joke among the elite. The joke was on them. As "Level 5" multiplying churches were birthed and then multiplied, in a short time the gospel began to cover entire nations.

Pastor and *The Message* author Eugene Peterson's version of Mark 6:14 gives us a fresh vision of what I hope and pray will literally happen in our world through multiplication. When the disciples return from their first multiplication mission, Mark reports these results, *"…The name of Jesus was on everyone's lips"* (*The Message*). May it be so!

3

First Editions

5 Traits of Biblical Multiplication

Most experiences in life grow duller with repetition. My first kiss set off fireworks. My 1,000th kiss was "nice." The first time I had Ben & Jerry's Cherry Garcia ice cream, I thought I had tasted Heaven. Now it still tastes good, but it also smacks of calories.

The book of Acts is *not* like that for me. Each time I read through its pages, a fresh fire of faith grips my spirit, and my "vision eyes" get bigger. For me, the inspired record of the first edition of *play thuno* is like listening to Handel's *Messiah* for the first time. I didn't have to be told to stand on the "Hallelujah Chorus" because I couldn't stay in my seat. My spirit pulled me straight out of my chair. The *Messiah* still does that for me. So does the book of Acts as it traces the journey of the first Level 5 multiplying church. Acts gives us key insights that help almost any willing church move towards Level 5.

Insight 1: Prayer positions us for multiplication.

After following the multiplication trail through the pages of Scripture, landing in Acts 1 primes us for an explosion ... or a dud. If the disciples do what Jesus instructed and modeled for them, you know there will be fireworks. If they try to do it the way of the Pharisees, their movement will fizzle out like an outdated Alka Seltzer.

Acts starts out with an emphasis on the church's weakness and the Spirit's power—the call to "wait" for the power so they can "witness" with power. Unless it is powered by the Holy Spirit, no strategy will be eternally effective. Consequently, the first *play thuno* team waits in prayer in the upper room. Through prayer, they position themselves for the power to multiply.

This reality hasn't changed. Recently, I was leading a meeting of pastors brainstorming on about how to move churches to multiply. I had scratched out 20 ideas on the board without one mention of prayer. When I wrote down "intense, faith-filled prayer," one pastor spoke up, "Oh, we assumed that already." I suggested his statement was too often the reality. Prayer is assumed instead of activated. Then we wonder why "Acts" type movement does not occur.

One of the classic moments in the story of our church is an "upper room" moment directly preceding my arrival. For years, the church had been plateaued with little to no conversion growth. The small group of saints was trying to keep the doors open. One of the lay leaders got desperate and rallied the church to a focused night of prayer. As the church was literally on their knees praying for souls, the back door suddenly opened and a stranger hesitantly walked down the aisle. Everyone turned to look at this ordinary-looking fellow.

"Is this a church meeting?" he asked.

The leader replied, "Yes. Can we help you in any way?"

The man's voice wobbled with emotion before he choked out, "Can you tell me how to become a Christian? I need Jesus."

Tony Cook became a follower of Christ that evening.

That night, prayer took on a new priority for our church. Hundreds of people have walked down that same aisle to receive Christ and become members. Hundreds have walked back out that same aisle to start new churches. In profound ways, each of our church plants can be traced to significant times of prayer.

Insight 2: Each individual has the potential to be a multiplier.

My friend, Guy, drove a local taxi for a living. As a nominal Christian, he was more interested in his taxi fares than the people who provided them. However, Guy had an encounter with the Holy Spirit resulting in an ignition of passion to share the gospel with his passengers. Soon, Guy was leading a Bible study with new converts and shortly thereafter became their pastor. Several other churches have now been birthed because of Guy's willingness to trust God to use his "ordinary" life. He still occasionally drives his taxi.

Have you ever really thought about the biblical truth that every Christian—*everyone* in the church you lead—carries the spark that could start the fire of a new church? Look at what Acts chapter 2 shows us about our call to go. The chapter starts with the sound of a tornado rushing through the house where they were gathered. Then in Acts 2:3, something profound happens. Don't miss this: "*They saw what seemed to be tongues of fire that separated and came to rest on each of them.*"

As they watched, one bundle of flame separated and distributed itself in individual flames over the head of each person gathered there. The *one* flame multiplied to become 120 individual flames. The message in the multiplied flames burns brightly. This power for mission was not just given to Peter and the 12 apostles. *Each* person was a flame carrier.

Ordinary, unnamed followers of Jesus received the message and the means of multiplication. The flame of truth and the fire of the Holy Spirit danced over their heads singing, "Go into all the world."

That same flame is dancing over your head, too. The Spirit empowers us with that same fire to carry light to our world. *You* were saved for this mission; *you* are called to pierce the darkness!

Today, the complexity of "doing church" often dampens the flame to start churches. Believers feel they must be able to preach, lead, counsel, negotiate leases, understand insurance, fundraise, chair boards, evangelize, visit hospitals, teach, run sound, shoot video, tweet and post before they could ever hope to begin a church. Feeling inadequate in the face of such apparent requirements quenches any spark of church planting. The Holy Spirit, however, is creative and empowering. "Doing church" can be reimagined and emancipated from complexities. The Spirit's anointing can unleash regular people.

Multiplication continues as God multiplies their one language (Aramaic) into many diverse languages, allowing all of the nationalities present in Jerusalem for the feast of Pentecost to hear and respond to the Truth.

I was once in a seminary class made up of students representing nine different nationalities. The professor had us sing the profoundly simple song, "Jesus Loves Me" in English, which we all spoke. Next, he had us sing it together again but this time in our individual "heart" language. I still remember how almost palpably the presence of God filled that classroom as we repeated the humble chorus through several times.

The Acts 2 messengers and their message were unified, but the delivery was diverse to reach the unique hearts of those listening. We see multiplication power when biblical truth is contextualized in a variety of languages. The timing of this outpouring of the Spirit was understandably significant to the spread of the gospel. This scene was like a revival at the United Nations. With so many nations gathered (Acts 2:5-11), Peter's redemptive message could be multiplied and distributed to much of the known world. As the Jerusalem pilgrims encountered the risen Christ through the Holy Spirit, they were empowered to carry the gospel truth back to the countries they traveled from.

No doubt, Peter's message set the stage for glorious addition to take place (Acts 2:41). On the first Pentecost, 3,000 people went public with their faith. They were "charter members" of this new Jesus church. As fantastic as this was, thankfully "addition" doesn't fill the rest of Acts. It was a beautiful and necessary jumpstart for the Church, but "multiplication" would soon take center stage. Addition would be vital, but the church was birthed to *play thuno*. This "game" was so essential that God went to extreme measures to see that the church did not become stuck in addition.

Insight 3: Multiplying leaders is key to multiplication.

The chronology of Acts is uncertain, but most scholars place Stephen's stoning in Acts 7 between 18 and 42 months after the Day of Pentecost. His death becomes a catalyst for the multiplication of the early church. For that first period, the new church seems a bit stuck in addition. Yes, the church is on fire with the Spirit, adding believers daily. The believers seem to be staying in Jerusalem, and God is blessing them by adding to their numbers.

However, it's not until Acts 6 when we see other believers coming to the forefront. Seven deacons of the church, including Stephen, are selected. For the first recorded time in the new church, there is a public multiplication of leadership. The immediate result of this multiplication is expansion and blessing: *"So the word of God spread. The number of disciples in Jerusalem increased rapidly, and a large number of priests became obedient to the faith"* (Acts 6:7). Once again, we encounter *plēthynō*, the Greek word translated "increased." Through multiplication of leadership, the church took a quantum leap forward.

Microsoft founder Bill Gates asserts, "As we look ahead into the next century, leaders will be those who empower others."[1] Leaders who move beyond instruction to empowerment will exert the most significant impact for the Kingdom. This multiplication of leadership declares two vital realities: "You can do it" and "I don't have to do it so I can do something more," which means much additional Kingdom work gets done.

I've illustrated this concept to our staff using a small plate and sugar. If you pour sugar on the plate, it will only pile up so high before it runs off the plate. No matter how fast or how much more sugar you pour, the pile will not rise any higher. The only solution is a larger plate. Increase the size of the base, and you increase the height of the pile. The plate or base is leadership. The more leaders we have, the larger our church can grow. More and more people can come our way, but they will not stick (pile higher) if we don't have an adequate number of leaders to care for them. Leadership multiplication becomes a key to higher addition.

Insight 4: Persecution can be a catalyst toward multiplication.

Regrettably, persecution would be the necessary whistle that started the serious *play thuno* game. With Stephen's stoning, the disciples scattered (Acts 8) taking the Spirit's fire with them. The disciples now seemed to get on track with the discipleship method Jesus had shown them. Acts 8:4 tells us that those who had been scattered preached the Word wherever they went. From village to village, they shared the Good News, discipling diverse people in various locations. Acts 8 offers one specific example of this gospel mission unfolding. Philip is sent to evangelize and baptize a high-ranking Ethiopian official on the Gaza road. Then Philip takes the Good News north, beginning in Azotus and then village-by-village continues on until he hits Caesarea.

In Acts 9, the unimaginable happens. Saul of Tarsus, the feared persecutor of the church, meets the One he hates and becomes the chief promoter of Jesus as Lord. Saul, soon called Paul, employs the same methods that Jesus taught his 12 apostles. Paul goes with partners and apprentices, preaching the gospel, making disciples, and multiplying churches.

Today, I increasingly hear groans concerning the degenerating cultural climate in America. I, too, grieve the loss of Sundays as church days, traditional two-parent families, the church as a social center of communities, Judeo-Christian ethics and Christian-friendly city councils. Yet I also experience an increasing sense of anticipation. The growing "resistance" to the Church is fostering a climate ripe for the multiplication of the Church. I sense the Church will become:

- an "any day" opportunity;
- the new spiritual family;
- the "third place" social spot for more people;
- an alternate lifestyle to the pains of immorality;
- and will move from a few dedicated buildings into diverse gathering places everywhere.

Church pain can lead to Kingdom gain. When our city council restricted the size of public gatherings by decreeing that 20 parking spaces were required for every 1,000 feet of assembly space, we were disillusioned. We had a tenth of the number of parking spots the new law had mandated. Our dreams of adding seats to our current location were shattered. That reality, however, helped give birth to our first church plant and subsequently a whole river of multiplication that flows through our city and now overseas.

'It Multiplied': The Why

I've always loved Acts 9:31: *"So the church throughout all Judea and Galilee and Samaria had peace and was being built up. And walking in the fear of the Lord and in the comfort of the Holy Spirit, it multiplied" (ESV)*.

Luke sums up the church's first season of multiplication. More importantly, he gets to the crux of *why* the church multiplied. Throughout the rest of this chapter, I want to look at the five traits of biblical multiplication Luke gives us in this verse by parsing out and studying the scripture. Note that Level 5 churches share all of these characteristics.

The "Big C" church (*"So the church throughout all Judea and Galilee and Samaria…"*)

Luke's language is profoundly simple and stunning—"the church throughout all Judea and Galilee and Samaria"—as if to declare that in every town and village in all three countries, there is really only one Church. This is the first time in Scripture that the universal, distinct but connected, unified, "Big C" church is clearly mentioned.

To develop a multiplying culture in our churches, as leaders we must be willing to prioritize the name of the King and the work of His Kingdom far above our own name and the work of our local church. Devoid of this "Kingdom view," our ministry grid will prioritize addition-growth in our church above the expansion of the "Big C" church.

Recently, I preached at the 50th anniversary of a church 10 miles away from ours. The church was packed, with a crowd of 500 people in attendance. Weekly, this place reverberates with energy, worship, outreach, servanthood and missions.

Eleven years earlier, it had almost been buried.

In 2004 I was on a conference call with our denominational leaders as they discussed the closing of the church and selling of the property. It was logical. The church was less than 40 people, and almost all were older than 70. The property was worth a few million dollars. However, our local church leadership and I had become deeply convicted of "Big C" church thinking. We offered to do whatever it took to revive this church.

At significant sacrifice to our local church, we sent money, leaders, workers and tithers to this dying church. At first, the situation looked tenuous, and we wondered if we had made a wise investment. But we hung on and even sent our own executive pastor there to lead full time. At this church's anniversary, I wept in gratitude as the manifestation of the power of "Big C" thinking was demonstrated so tangibly in front of me.

Just as significant was the lesson for our church. It's not about our church; it's about His Church!

The "Big C" church – a Kingdom understanding and priority upon the universal Church more than our local church.

The "Conflict-less" church ("...*had peace*")

The Church that had experienced significant persecution at the start of Acts 8 entered into a different season at the end of Acts 9. Scholars attribute this to the conversion of the chief prosecutor (Saul) and to political changes in leadership. The church enjoyed a relative calm, allowing for some infrastructure to develop among the gatherings of believers.

Although not explicit, something important is implicitly communicated here. The Church was not on a boisterous and vocal mission to right the wrongs of the dominant Roman culture. By not publically demonstrating against the deceived values of Roman rule, the Church did not unnecessarily invite the reprisals of Rome. Certainly they were praying for and addressing issues of justice and mercy, however, the primary means of transforming the dehumanizing culture was not through political battle. Rather, the Church focused on changing the hearts of people with the gospel. Conversion by conversion, the Church undermined the strongholds of societal ills.

Notice that I did't call this the "Conflict-free" church. There is no such church or place. The church will always rub a Christ-less culture the wrong way. It's like the little boy who was told he was petting the cat the wrong direction. To which he replied, "No I'm not. The cat just needs to turn around." The church that compromises and placates soon disqualifies herself for the title of "church," especially since we are the *ekklessia*—the ones "called out" from the culture. We cannot escape conflict. We will often rub the cat's fur the wrong way, but we can refrain from "pulling the cat's tail."

Too many churches unwisely invite conflict. Known more for what they are "against" than what they are "for," their social agendas become impediments to their gospel agendas. They hobble, or even shoot, their horse of multiplication with these kinds of priorities. It's nearly impossible to *play thuno* if you're playing politics.

I think about a large church I know of that has experienced, in my opinion, the downside of a social issue/political priority. With their state of the art facilities and their prominent public voice, the church has grown. Raising the hood of the church, however, reveals some engine problems. The church appears to have grown by appealing to a very narrow slice of people who are as angry about the same issues as the church is. This particular church is now losing momentum and is far from their forgotten goal of multiplication.

There is another indirect aspect of the phrase "the church … had peace." Ephesians 4:3 brings it to light: "Make every effort to keep the unity of the Spirit through the bond of peace." Paul understands the underlying dynamics of an effective church. If the people of the church are not pursuing peace internally, they cannot minister peace externally. If the church is warring among themselves, they cannot carry peace to the community. Unity and peace fuel the engine of multiplication.

I recall counseling a married couple that was seeking to have their first child but having trouble getting pregnant. I knew it was a high-conflict marriage. They talked about various medical treatments to increase their chances of becoming pregnant. I delicately suggested we give the Lord another six months and during that time work on increasing the peace in their marriage. They actually followed through and as you might guess, when peace reigned in their marriage, reproduction occurred.

Being clear about our values and mission—not intense navel gazing—is the primary path to church peace. I've known many churches that spend months or years in self-examination only to end up more divided in the end. If the "where" (where are we headed/vision) and the "what" (what are our values) are in focus, then peace generally results.

Because the church is comprised of people like me (and you), it will never be "conflict-*free*" until Jesus returns. But the church can be "conflict-*less*." The mission can be so compelling that little time or attention is left over for pursuing conflict.

When I came to Light & Life and began to make sweeping changes, the air filled with the stench of criticism. One of the most helpful moments of "air freshening" came when the mother of the church, Mama Beverly, stood up to publicly support me. Her words remain one of my favorite all-time quotes: "If we would all get busy rowing the boat, we wouldn't have time to rock it!"

The "Conflict-less" church – a passionate emphasis on the gospel mission of Jesus, which reduces friction within the church and with the culture outside the church.

The "Construction" church *("...and was being built up")*

My small hometown on the Kansas prairies has not been known for vibrant churches. So I was shocked when I shared a Facebook post about making a new friend, Andy Addis, leader of the multisite Crosspoint Church in Hutchison, Kansas, and started to get comments from hometown acquaintances: "Hey, that's my Pastor." "Love my church home." "I've grown so much here." As I pressed into what was happening in this church, so much of it was about being Christocentric, having biblical clarity and cultivating authentic family community. The Church is "being built up," and Crosspoint is one of the fastest multiplying churches in Mid-America.

Two essentials in church multiplication are doctrinal clarity and loving relationships. Passion for truth and for the church family creates an environment conducive for growth and planting. The third phrase of Acts 9:31 is resplendent with beauty and meaning. One of Jesus' most famous guarantees comes in light of this description. In Matthew 16:18, Jesus promises His apprentices he would "build His church." Here in Acts 9:31, Christ's vow is fulfilled.

The same Greek word, *oikodomeō*, used in Matthew, is used here in Acts. This brilliant Greek word is a "construction" term representing the idea of building upon a foundation. The foundation of Christ forms the unshakeable location, but on top of that foundation sits a building. While the foundation (Christ) is the most essential part of the structure (the church), it is unseen, below ground level. The Church—the body of Christ—makes the unseen presence of the foundation visible to the world.

You've probably heard the construction phrase "raise the walls"—when the framed walls are raised up and secured to the foundation of a house. At this point, the builder provides temporary support for the walls because the next step is "strengthening" the raised walls. This strengthening happens as the builder begins to "tie the building together" with the other component parts.

In the same way, "raising" and "strengthening" the walls are part of "building the church." How does this happen practically? The progression of the early church gives us some clues. As the church's knowledge and love for the teachings of Jesus grew, the church in Acts constructed its theology upon the foundation of Christ. As the church began to apply Jesus' teachings to their daily lives, they began to be visible both within and outside the church. And. as the church increased in their understanding of their attachment to the person and mission of Christ, they carried out the missional lifestyle that Christ's church was born for. The walls were raised and "strengthened."

I recently observed an enthusiastic church with a rapidly growing number of 20-somethings making their way through the church's doors. These young adults were intense about their worship experience and serving their community. It was beautiful—and shaky. From my perspective, the church was failing to take doctrinal truth seriously. The walls were not well attached to the foundation. It seemed that as easily as these newcomers blew into the church, they could blow right back out.

On the other hand, I visited a church that was slowly shriveling away. Their walls were securely fastened to the foundation every few inches. They were solid but stuck. Accurate but dead doctrine. Expressions of the heart of Christ to their community were non-existent. They intended to hang on until Jesus came, but Jesus was outlasting them, and they were dying off.

The "strengthening" that happened in Acts 9:31 was carried out not only through doctrine and mission, but also through the context of the family of believers (unlike today's American church where individualism reigns). The church of Acts was conceived of in "familial" terms. Think about the references to "brothers and sisters." However, you can be sure that that this "familial" nature was not the clannish, cliquish, internally focused holy huddle that makes up many churches in America. It was a family living on an urgent mission. These family relationships were not used to keep individuals close to home but rather to launch them forth from the security of a loving home family. As these family-like relationships deepened, the church was "strengthened."

Of course the raising and strengthening are never complete. Whatever phase our church is in (pre-launch, post-launch, mid-life, etc.), we must always pay attention to and monitor the construction process. When we begin to sit back, the results (or lack of) begin to show just like the century-old house we live in. It deserves and requires ongoing attention.

The "Construction" church – building a love for, and understanding and application of the doctrines and mission of Jesus—carrying out that mission in the context of deepening relationships.

The "Consecrated" church (*"…And walking in the fear of the Lord …"*)

It may seem odd to find an Old Testament phrase in this summary description of the church of Acts. Isn't "fear of the Lord" a tad bit antiquated for this new season of "what a friend we have in Jesus" and "Jesus, lover of my soul"? The first-century Church was living in the new age of freedom and Holy Spirit liberty. Yet, one of the defining marks of the kind of church that multiplies is a high regard for God's opinion.

The ESV translates this part of verse 31 *"walking in the fear of the Lord"* while the NIV says, *"living in the fear of the Lord."* The lives of these early Christians were permeated by an awe of who Jesus was and a carefulness to please Him in every matter. Yes, this healthy fear filtered the words and actions of the church, but it also reached below the surface to their motivations. This was not cringing fear, wringing its hands with insecurity and uncertainty. Neither was it a superstitious fear seeking not to disturb an angry God. Nor was it a legalistic fear leading to human-generated, religious rules. This was a glorious fear born of Godward desire, a devotion to treat God as real with a real opinion.

Of course, Ananias' story in Acts 5 advances this Acts 9:31 "fear." Acts 5:5 cites the first occurrence of the word "fear" in the book of Acts. It comes after Ananias had treated the Lord like He didn't really concern Himself with the average believer. After failing to "fear" God, Ananias falls down dead, causing a great "fear" to fall on all of the church. The message was clear—motives matter, secrets aren't secret, and you don't mess around with the mission. The mission is a life and death matter. This was a purifying moment for the church. You can't *play thuno* with mixed motives, hidden agendas or selfish ambitions. A church "walking in the fear of the Lord" is the kind of church that can learn to "run in the mission of the Lord." It is the type of culture that may give rise to multiplication.

In my experience, church elder boards can be either the ultimate roadblock or a great blessing to a church's multiplication efforts. At our church, our board has been incredibly faith-filled and visionary. However, there have been tough seasons. One of our board members, Sam, was an expert at helping companies be profitable. So once he began to do the math of how much our church planting efforts were costing us financially. Sam had serious pushback. His concerns started to spread to other board members.

I began to address these worries through explanation, information resourcing and especially through prayer. One day, Sam came to me and confessed, "Pastor, I have come to apologize and repent. God convicted me that I was allowing my fears instead of my faith to rule my reasoning. I know that's sin. I know God's bigger than that, and I care about God's opinion, so you've got my backing."

This reverence for the Lord is the breeding ground for the humility that multiplication cultures require. When a person fears the circumstances more than they revere God, multiplication becomes difficult. Obedience often requires sacrifice, and sacrifice is generally scary: *If we give this money, or if I speak up, or if I serve all weekend, or if I love this person, or if I give away part of my church to start a new church, it might hurt.* Exactly. However in that moment of pain, we discover that obeying God has its own reward. Fearing the Lord above all else brings a freedom like nothing else.

Growing up, I owned an Australian Shepherd named Freckles. She was a brilliant canine who became a one-master dog. I loved her, and she reciprocated. Whenever I was home, Freckles was by my side, watching my every move, seeking a way to please me. My opinion mattered to her. I couldn't play tackle football without locking her inside the house because she would attack anyone who dared to tackle me. I had disciplined her but never mistreated her. She repaid me with consecrated devotion. My voice was her command, and I only wanted the best for my four-legged friend. Her "fear" was birthed from love and led to an attentiveness that seems like a good picture of the kind of reverence I want to give to God.

I like what *My Utmost for His Highest* author Oswald Chambers says about fearing God: "The remarkable thing about God is that when you fear God, you fear nothing else, whereas if you do not fear God, you fear everything else."[2]

The church that is most deeply secure in the love of God is the church that will fear the Lord most—fear generated by the knowledge of how good God is. Disobedience means we miss the blessing God has prepared for us. When the Spirit directs you to send, to sacrifice, to give, to multiply, the more frightening alternative is to disobey.

The "Consecrated church" – acute sensitivity to God's opinion of our motives and deeds, both individually and collectively.

The "Comforted church" *("…and in the comfort of the Holy Spirit")*

The church in Acts was walking or living in the comfort or encouragement of the Holy Spirit's active partnership with them. Some Bible translations emphasize "comfort," others "encouragement." But the crucial reality is the engaging presence of the Holy Spirit. The church was not alone on this mission—internal comfort and encouragement paired with external power and boldness. As a result, the church became a gospel witness producing visible results and taking the form of multiplication.

The early church experienced a continual breeze of the mighty wind that had blown through the day of Pentecost:

The Spirit *dwelled* among them and upon them.

The Spirit *picked them up* when they fell down.

The Spirit *healed* them when their hearts were wounded.

The Spirit *placed His arm around them* when they seemed forsaken on the journey.

The Spirit *breathed courage* into them to dream, to take risks, and to reach outside their comfort zone.

The Spirit *infused direction* into their daily encounters with nonbelievers.

The Spirit *gave birth* to new churches in new villages and towns.

The book of Acts is a continual reminder that ordinary people filled with the Spirit can take on extraordinary exploits for God. Time and again, I've watched churches of all stripes and denominations come alive to the Holy Spirit. As we place greater priority upon ushering in the presence and power of the Holy Spirit, the church exponentially increases. Faith grows. Vision burns. Energy soars. Commitment deepens. Barriers bust. A church that has been unable to give birth suddenly finds itself pregnant.

It is just like Luke to tie the Holy Spirit and multiplication together. A few books before in his gospel, he did the same thing in the first chapter of his book. Mary was a childless virgin when Gabriel stopped in with his announcement that she would soon give birth to a son. The angels gave her a vision of multiplication she'd never fathomed before. However, being a pragmatic teenage girl, she asked, "How will this be since I am a virgin?" (Luke 1:34).

"The Holy Spirit will come on you, and the power of the Most High will overshadow you ..." (Luke 1:35). Mary's response indicated willingness and faith: "I am the Lord's servant, may your word to me be fulfilled" (Luke 1:38). Nine months later, Jesus was born. Multiplication occurred.

When vision, willingness and faith combine and are then "overshadowed" with the Holy Spirit, multiplication happens. God is calling for servants today who have a "Mary" heart, individuals who catch the vision of giving birth and being multiplied; who fully yield themselves to God's service without constricting concern for their own reputation; and who exercise faith that something beyond their own ability can happen through the power of God. When the Spirit finds a church with that "Mary" heart, He then can overshadow it with His presence and together they can *play thuno.*

This "overshadowing" is rare today. Believing that the right "methodology" is more important than the right "partnership" with the Spirit, too many leaders and churches are often too interested in the quickest way to the spotlight and thus forfeit the "overshadowing" of the Spirit. Interestingly, the Greek word translated "overshadow" is used five times in the New Testament, three of which relate to the transfiguration of Jesus. Matthew describes a "bright cloud covering them" (Matt. 17:5). In each of these three cases, God's voice first rivets attention to Jesus by saying, "This is my Son." Jesus is identified, focused on, and exalted. Then the voice gives a command: "Listen to Him."

Those who see Jesus are required to listen to Him.

"Overshadowing" by the Holy Spirit increases our focus and our following of Jesus. We lose sight of our own reputation and glory, swallowed up in the glorious revelation of who Jesus is and how worthy of all praise He really is. In that posture, we have a passion to serve Him. I think of it as the Samuel experience: "Speak Lord, for your servant is listening." (1 Sam. 3:10).

Today, the Spirit still "overshadows" us and spotlights Jesus—yearning for servants who let Jesus be Jesus and are eager to listen to Him and live out His direction. This type of Spirit-breathed comfort results in the multiplication of new believers and churches. This is Acts 9:31's declaration. When the Church was walking in the comfort, encouragement and partnership of the Holy Spirit, it multiplied. Throughout the rest of the book of Acts, we see this pattern repeated. The Church is gathered, built up, consecrated, empowered by the Spirit, and then some believers are sent out to *play thuno*.

When our church was a small struggling group of believers, the vision of multiplication was nowhere to be seen. We were a Level 1 church fighting subtraction. However, Acts 9:31 thinking began to grip us. We began to see the broader body of Christ (Big C), we focused on unity and the simplicity of the gospel (Conflict-less), we asked God to build us up (Construction), we fasted, prayed and sought to obey (Consecrated), and we begged the Holy Spirit to "overshadow" us (Comforted).

The results have been humbling. We've moved from Level 1 to a solid Level 4 and are journeying towards Level 5. We have much to learn and implement, but the Spirit is working.

The "Comforted church" – radical dependency upon the active presence, power and guidance of the Holy Spirit.

4

Two Roles in the Game

10 Telling Questions for Multiplication

O n April 3, 1860 when the Pony Express made its first ride, few
realized then how this new innovation would revolutionize
communication in the American West. The process took some
determined manpower and real horsepower, but the work was worth it.

A rider would mount his horse at the starting point in St. Joseph,
Missouri, and gallop as hard as the horse could run for about 10 miles.
Then the rider would switch to a fresh horse that had been prepared at
a "swing station," and the mail would move forward. Some 157 stations
later, your letter arrived in Sacramento, California.

After every eight to 10 "swing stations" was a "home station" where not
only the horse but also the rider was traded and a fresh rider was sent
forward. Using this "send and be sent" method of communication, mail
could travel from Missouri to the West Coast in an unbelievable span
of just 10 days. If a wife in St. Joseph had a baby on May 1, her gold-
mining husband in California could learn the good news by May 11.

This new model was exponentially faster than the standard means of
carrying the news. However, the process required that two essential roles
be filled: "home station keeper" and "express rider." Both jobs required

courage, but each demanded different gifts and talents. The home station keeper was vital to this communication operation. He often lived in remote areas, establishing a home base far from the safety of other homes. The station keeper's success was not based on how many riders he kept, but how many riders he sent. As soon as a rider came in, he sent another one on their way. As soon as that fresh rider was out the door, the station keeper was busy getting the next rider ready to go.

You can picture the station keeper getting water for the rider to clean up with, fixing dinner for him, making up a bed, mending wounds and treating sore muscles worn out from the journey. The station keeper was probably good at repairing or creating equipment needed for the next ride. He equipped the riders to do the work of carrying the message.

The other vital role in the Pony Express was the "express rider." This brave soul was born to "go," to ride into new territory because the news was needed there. This was a dangerous job with no assurances as to what he might encounter over the next hill or around the next bend. He faced constant danger of being attacked, or falling, or dehydrating in the heat, or freezing in the cold, or getting lost along the way.

The calling of the rider was clear—to be sent forward with the news.

When the station keeper fulfilled his role of "sending" and the "express rider" carried out his role of "being sent," then, and only then, could the mail travel rapidly to everyone who needed it.

"Sender" and "Sent One"

Play thuno requires two primary roles: sender and sent one. Every church needs station keepers and express riders. Station keepers create a healthy environment conducive to the equipping of those who will be going. Express riders prepare so that they are ready to lead a new church plant or help someone else do so.

Every church aspiring to be a Level 5 multiplying church should instill two sets of questions in their corporate and individual culture:

"Sender" questions:

1. Who are we equipping to be sent out from us?
2. How are we preparing them?
3. Where will they be sent?
4. What resources will we send them with?
5. Are we keeping the vision of multiplication clear?

"Sent ones" questions:

1. Is it my time to go?
2. How am I preparing to go?
3. Is there a place I am feeling called to go?
4. Am I arranging my resources to be ready to go?
5. Am I multiplying where I am while waiting to be sent?

The Antioch Example

The church at Antioch knew how to *play thuno.* Acts 13:1-4 describes this kind of "Pony Express" church: *"Now in the church at Antioch there were prophets and teachers: Barnabas, Simeon called Niger, Lucius of Cyrene, Manaen (who had been brought up with Herod the tetrarch) and Saul. While they were worshiping the Lord and fasting, the Holy Spirit said, 'Set apart for me Barnabas and Saul for the work to which I have called them.' So after they had fasted and prayed, they placed their hands on them and sent them off. The two of them, sent on their way by the Holy Spirit, went down to Seleucia and sailed from there to Cyprus."*

Clearly, the Antioch church enjoyed the prophetic and teaching gifts of the individuals listed here in Acts 13. But this church was not content to be fed, built up and stirred up. They were not okay with being a Level 3 church of addition.

Too many churches today are content to simply feed on the words of the prophets and teachers. I daresay the glut of inspiration and information without application is smothering the apostolic impetus in churches. The Church seems more interested in napping than riding hard with the message.

Acts 13:2 implies that the Antioch church worshiped and fasted to hear the voice of the Holy Spirit's guidance. They probably asked God, "Who do we send? When do we send them? Where do we send them?" As the church fasted, they clearly heard the Holy Spirit's direction to send out their best leaders. The Antioch church was to become a sending church where apostolic gifts were empowered and released.

I truly believe that most churches and church leaders want to do something great for God. Unfortunately, only a precious few want to do what it takes to seek God. Their investment in fasting, prayer and worship is quite small. Consequently, there is little hearing from God. Significant spiritual steps forward require kneeling first. Our spiritual hearing dramatically improves simply by lowering the elevation of our heads.

When our church decided to start planting a series of churches, we knew this was so far beyond us that we would have to take our prayer levels far past where they currently were. We called our church to a 40-day fast,. which kicked my behind since I decided to fast all solid food. A couple of weeks into it, I could smell a French fry from 200 yards away.

Our church did prayer walks, went to the highest point of our city and prayed, drove through neighborhoods praying, rode bicycles around the 36-mile perimeter of our city praying, and had all-night prayer meetings.

We weren't legalistically seeking God's favor, but we were sincerely seeking more of His presence and power for this sending mission. We were a Level 3 church of addition trying to break the magnetic pull to stay that way. We needed a breakthrough to move toward Level 4 and start reproducing.

God answered our prayers in unexpected ways. The Holy Spirit eventually said, "Set apart Larry and JR (our former youth pastor and one of our first church planters) for this work I've called them to." Like Antioch, our church began to give birth to new churches. We learned that the more adept a church becomes at "sending," the more impact that church will make for the mission of Christ.

The Necessity of Being Sent

Once the Antioch church identified the messengers, the church returned to fasting and prayer: *"So after they had fasted and prayed, they placed their hands on them and sent them off"* (Acts 13:3). This time, their prayers seemed focused on empowerment and preparation for the mission. They responded to the Spirit's initial communication by confirming it, surrounding it, and then supporting it with still more prayer.

These people were serious about multiplication! Their actions indicate the very real possibility that when we choose to become a "sending" church, we can expect spiritual warfare. What happened at Antioch was the last thing the devil ever wants to see—a church on its knees getting ready to multiply. Nothing causes Satan to tremble like a church determining to be a "sending" church and then mixing that direction with intercession.

The next scene in the Antioch church pictures Paul and Barnabas in the middle of the church surrounded by the elders, prophets, teachers and people. A dozen or more hands are touching the two leaders, and prayers of commitment, anointing, empowerment, protection and blessing are launched to Heaven on their behalf. Then they themselves are launched into a new adventure. The church commissions them to, "go and multiply disciples, workers, leaders and churches."

The "sent ones" set off on their church-planting venture. I love the affirmation that Acts 13:4 offers: *"sent on their way by the Holy Spirit."* The passage suggests a question: Who sent them? The church (13:3) or the Holy Spirit (13:4)? How about both? The Holy Spirit through the church sent them. The church was behind them, and the Spirit was with them. With that double assurance, Paul and Barnabus boldly headed out for the mission of Christ.

I'm dismayed by how many church planters "go" without being "sent." They claim the direction and empowerment of the Holy Spirit and while I'm quite slow to doubt them, I do fear for them and the churches they plant. If I can be bold, these "unsent" planters are seeking to build a church with one arm tied behind their back. "One-armed" churches usually go up slow, or crooked, or both. One of the leading pastors in our city boldly asks new planters, "Who sent you and why?" He understands the perils of trying to build with one arm.

Church planting is challenging enough even when both the Spirit and the church send you. To go without one or the other is foolhardy and often emits a faint scent of rebellion or at least independence. I always counsel young planters that being sent with a blessing, an anointing, a spiritual covering, and an intercessory team behind you is the safest and most productive way to "go."

The "Sending" School

As Paul goes about pioneering new churches, he seeks to go to Asia but the Holy Spirit forbids him (Acts 16:6). Then he specifically tries to go to Bithynia and again gets the stop sign from the Holy Spirit (Acts

16:7). Immediately after the Spirit halts him, Paul receives a vision, often referred to as the Macedonian Call. In that portion of his missionary journey, he establishes churches in Philippi, Thessalonica, Berea, and Corinth. Great work for the gospel, but what about Asia?

Eventually Paul ends up in Ephesus. The work is going well until a group of people begin to "malign the Way" (Acts 19:9), and Paul is forced to relocate to the school of Tyrannus where he can teach the disciples who were coming to faith in Christ.

We have no idea how many disciples were trained at the school, but it seems to have become a church planting school, a "sending station." What we do know is that what Paul did in the Ephesus church and specifically at this school had far-reaching impact. Acts 19:10 informs us: *"This went on for two years, so that all the Jews and Greeks who lived in the province of Asia heard the word of the Lord."*

Don't miss the implication here. Paul could have gone into Asia and spread the gospel to one city, one church plant at a time (similar to a Level 4 reproducing church). Instead, God stopped him, eventually took him to Ephesus, and equipped him to start a prolific "sending station" (a Level 5 multiplying church). The planters that were sent out from Ephesus took the gospel everywhere, creating a "multiplication movement." Paul learned to *play thuno*, resulting in all of Asia hearing the gospel. Paul learned both roles of "sent one" and "sender." Playing both roles with excellence made him a dynamic influencer.

My prayer is that many more "sending schools" would be raised up. They may take the form of internships, residencies, church-planting schools, church-planting networks, Christian colleges or seminary programs, etc. These schools, with a healthy rootedness in or with local churches, can help reach our entire nation with the gospel.

Notice that Paul's school was not a four-year program. The school only lasted a total of two years, and students didn't stay for two years. When they were ready, they were sent. I believe we often over-teach and under-reach. After just enough training, Jesus and Paul sent their students into the field. But the coaching and training didn't stop. It continued in the field. The actual learning took place more in the field than in the classroom.

Movements happen when the motivation is strong enough and the message and methods are simple enough for all to play the game. *Play thuno* is not a complex game, but we must learn to play both roles, "senders" and "sent ones," if we hope to be a church that rapidly carries the Good News to waiting people.

5

Strategies of the Game

5 Life-Giving Principles for Multiplication

Merle Robbins loved cutting hair and playing cards. One day in 1971 while sitting in his barbershop Merle had a brainstorm for a new kind of card game. He named it UNO, and soon his friends were playing it with him. Robbins' family put together an $8,000 investment and had 5,000 games made. They all sold.

Later, Robbins sold UNO for $50,000 and royalties of 10 cents for each game to a funeral home owner named Robert Tezak. UNO ended up in a funeral home office, surrounded by death. Some people probably thought Merle had played the fool by selling his game for a mere $50,000. But Robbins knew he didn't have the resources to grow the game much larger. He knew that when he released it to Tezak, his game could grow and multiply. Remember that Robbins had also negotiated a 10-cent royalty—a return based on multiplication instead of addition.

Since that sale to Tezak, over 200 million UNO games have been sold. If Robbins still has his royalty deal, his $50,000 selling price has been eclipsed by the $20 million and counting he has collected since. Robbins' big deal of selling 5,000 games is miniscule compared to the 200 million games that were waiting in one stack of UNO cards.

Every church and every Christian leader has "Level 5" multiplication potential, but almost always they settle for Level 3 addition. Most of them simply don't know *how* to move into multiplication.

5 Strategies to *Play Thuno*

As I have spent the last 16 years "planting" or "sending" churches, I've learned a great deal. Of course my biggest lesson is how much I still need to learn. But through my education, experiences, mistakes and observations, I've discovered what I believe are five basic strategies to *play thuno,* regardless of the size or model of church. Using an acrostic for T.H.U.N.O, we can see these five life-giving principles essential to becoming a Level 5 multiplying church.

T-Think multiplication not addition.

Level 5 churches have re-engineered their thinking and practice around multiplication.

When I began pastoring, my passion was to have the biggest church possible. Each person attending represented a "win." I certainly wanted them to know and grow in Jesus, but I certainly didn't want to them to actually *go* for Jesus. "Going" would mean they'd leave our church, which would hinder the vision I was trying to build.

I've since realized that our affection sets our direction. What we love is what we will shove everything else aside for. My affection used to be addition, a Level 3 church. My vision was to grow a megachurch. Something new, however, has taken root in my heart. While I still pray for new people to "come to" our church, I intercede even harder for people to "go from" our church. My mind is set on multiplication more than addition, which changes how we approach almost everything.

Multiplication thinking changes the scoreboard. Imagine if we redesigned the game of basketball so that every time a team had an "assist," that team would score five points. Think about how something like that would change the whole game. The team wouldn't just be shooting; they'd be looking to help one of their teammates score. The highest scorers, the stars of the game, would be the best passers, those who "sent" the ball to others.

What if we applied this concept to the church world? The most celebrated "heroes" would not be those leading the biggest churches, the ones majoring in addition. Instead, the real game-changers would be those leaders and churches helping start churches, focusing on multiplication.

Ultimately, this is fourth-generation thinking. When Paul wrote Timothy, he urged him to train some faithful disciples who would, in turn, train up disciples. Paul launched Timothy, who was to launch some faithful disciples, who were to launch others. When you train someone to focus on fourth-generation thinking, you dig in deep to reveal this multiplication passion within them, and then push out this passion beyond themselves, past their disciples, all the way to the fourth generation. That is some strong DNA! It changes the way you train your disciples. They are no longer recruiters for your church but instead multipliers for the Kingdom.

At the great-grandchild level, multiplication begins to take off exponentially. Think about it. If a parent is still living and is attending the baby shower of their great-grandchild's newest baby, you know their family reunions are going to be huge. You know that family name will likely be spread all over the nation.

To take on a multiplication mindset in your church, you, the leader, must move to a higher level of trusting God as your source.

Multiplication is not multi-level marketing with residuals. It is trusting God to replace the lost income through new converts and other believers (addition working with multiplication). You must deeply believe that you can't out-give God.

At Light & Life, we have given away as much as 25 percent of our monthly income by sending out tithers to church plants. Has it been scary? Quite. Has the timing always worked? Not on our calendar. Has God always been faithful? Absolutely. Each year since we started planting churches, we have ended with greater annual income than the previous year.

Thinking multiplication over addition reorients your church's mentality in radical Kingdom ways. It is a Romans 12:2 phenomenon in which our minds are renewed and transformed from the common corporate practices of this world into a supernatural abundance mentality. The fear of scarcity is replaced with faith in God's ability.

H-Honor Holy Spirit empowerment.
Level 5 churches radically depend on the ministry of the Spirit.

Multiplication is a work of the Holy Spirit. This statement may seem self-evident and unnecessary. It is not. Churches that choose to pursue Level 5 will need to develop a far deeper reliance upon the work and power of the Holy Spirit.

When we honor the Holy Spirit, we exercise bold faith because our God is big. My Kenyan friend, Oscar Muriu, in a tongue-in-cheek expression, exhorts us to, "pray prayers that make God sweat!" We dishonor the Holy Spirit with small dreams or an over-dependency upon our plans, cleverness or excellence. But "honoring" is evidenced by a whole new level of prayerfulness. The Acts church started at a prayer meeting. The church multiplies through prayer, which ushers in the Spirit's wind, fire and communication (Acts 2).

Often my international friends that have started hundreds of churches laugh when I ask them, "What exact steps are you following to produce such results?" I want the secret formula, the silver bullet. Usually, they say something like, "You Americans always want to reduce the Spirit's power into a strategy. You don't need more strategy; you need more Spirit."

Our books will never change the world. Our latest research won't reach people. Our conferences won't convert the globe. Only the Holy Spirit can spread spiritual fire. For you academics, we need an ecclesiology shaped by our pneumatology. In other words, the Spirit can't be added to our reliance upon ourselves. In the early church, multiplication happened as they honored, prioritized, sought, obeyed and trusted in the Spirit. Plain and simple, Jesus is the head of the Church, and He wants to pass on His guidance through the Holy Spirit. When we go to where the Spirit is leading, we soon find that the He has already been there working ahead of us and because of His "legwork," we can move into that place with much more fruitfulness.

When one of our church planters, Brian Warth, was trying to decide which area to plant in, he continued to seek the Spirit for direction. He kept hearing, "No, don't go there," but finally got a "yes" from the Spirit to come to Long Beach. Next, he looked for a place to hold worship services. Again, he kept getting "no's." But the Spirit instructed him to keep calling one particular church office again and again even though he received no answer and no call back when he left messages.

Brian discovered that, although this church had a large building, the congregation had diminished to a handful of elderly saints. The office was never open. At this point, he reached the end of his perseverance but felt distinctly prompted by the Spirit to make one last call. The phone rang repeatedly. Just as he was ready to hang up, one of the aged deacons happened to be at the church office that day and answered. Today, three years later, Brian leads a large thriving church in an amazing church facility that was sold to them at an unbelievably low price. They have just commissioned their first church planter.

The Holy Spirit inspires faith to believe God for greater harvest. When you pray fervently for the Spirit's power to be released upon ordinary people, your point of reference changes. No longer are you expecting results based on the talents of the individual or the brilliance of the strategy. Rather, you anticipate and prepare for results because you expect the Spirit to move. Honoring the Holy Spirit removes the focus from star players and makes every saint a conduit of the mission.

U-Unleash ordinary disciples.

Level 5 churches see their ordinary congregants as world changers.

If you're going to *play thuno*, realize that there is no "bench." Every team member is on the field every minute of the game until the final buzzer sounds. If you play "addition," you will find huge "benches." Addition is a game designed to help players double as spectators. But multiplication demands burning the benches and helping people get in the game from day one. *Play thuno* has a position for everyone and believes everyone can make a significant contribution to winning the "game."

Philip, the evangelist, is my model for "ordinary" disciples. He wasn't one of the 12 apostles. In fact, he's not even mentioned until Acts 6 when there is an election for "table waiters" to help out the widows. Philip is nominated as one full of the Spirit and wisdom. He was willing to serve and began his ministry as an administrator and caregiver. But Philip was destined for more. His heart was to see the lost meet Jesus and to see the Church multiply. He believed the Holy Spirit would use him, and over the next pages of Acts we see a deliverance ministry, a healing ministry, an evangelistic ministry, and a missionary ministry flow out of Philip's surrender. He also raised four daughters who practiced the ministry of the Word.

Scripture tells us that the Holy Spirit desires to take ordinary believers to a whole new level of impact. If we're honest, too often our vision for our church members is to see them pass out bulletins, bake cookies, collect the offering, attend church workdays and perhaps serve on the church finance board. But God built them to change the world. It's like keeping a racing boat in a park pond. We were saved for more than giving kiddy rides on a pond.

In his reformation, Martin Luther used 1 Peter 2:9—"… you are royal priests …"—as a key truth explaining, "In this way we are all priests, as many of us as are Christians." We must introduce people to Christ *and* to their true vocation—priesthood. When your paradigm changes to multiplication, the priests get to do priestly stuff. They begin to believe they were created and saved to multiply the church and change the world.

This past Sunday, our drummer shared about leading the lead singer of a world-famous rock band to Jesus just three days before he died last week. Drumming is a great ministry, but helping someone surrender to Jesus, now that is priestly work.

I've been convicted time and time again when I watched people who were sitting on the sidelines at our church go with one of our church-planting teams and turn into dynamic "priestly" leaders. We had them handing out bulletins, and now they're laying hands on the sick and seeing miracles. They are teaching, discipling, evangelizing, interceding. Multiplication placed the demand and the expectation on them, and they rose up to their priestly calling.

Perhaps the simplest way to lose at *play thuno* is to complicate it. Using sophisticated game plays and overly complex strategies leads to beautiful versions of *play thuno* that ultimately lead to defeat. It's the K.I.S.S. (Keep It Spirit-Filled & Simple) strategy that wins this game. As Alan Briggs, the director of Frontline Church Planting, says, "Jesus never sent out the scribes and Pharisees. They knew too much and obeyed too little."

We need to keep learning, but it must be the kind of learning that leads to what Albert Einstein called "simplicity on the other side of complexity."[1]

"Hear and obey" discipleship impacts the world and multiplies the church. If new believers of average intelligence with no formal theological education can't be unleashed as the star players on your team, then your game plan is misguided. This "unleashing" must include the "equipping" that Ephesians 4:12 emphasizes. Skills, tools and provisions will empower the ordinary person to serve in an effective Kingdom role.

My wife and I recently escaped Hurricane Patricia. Deb and I had joined our friends in Puerto Vallarta for five days of resting and writing at the Grand Mayan Resort. Three days into our time there, we learned that the most powerful hurricane ever measured was headed right for us. We had a choice to make: Do we drive our rental car inland eight hours to Guadalajara, or do we stay and try to help in what would surely be a tragic natural disaster? Our hearts told us to stay. But when we saw how we were equipped, we thought differently. We had flip-flops and beachwear. We were prepared for resort living instead of a rescue mission. With that reality check, we escaped to relative safety.

Often Christians are told to go on a rescue mission, but pastors have only provided flip-flops and beachwear. We are raising up disciples who are trained for their Christian resorts but not for the rescue mission in their neighborhood. As you begin to see your church filled with "priests" instead of just "people," I'm confident your multiplication imagination will be ignited. As you properly equip and release these ordinary disciples, you'll begin to unleash movement-making potential.

N-Nurture a neighborhood.

Level 5 churches practice a compassion-driven, missional, neighborly approach to multiplication.

To *play thuno*, you must be on the right field. In case you're wondering, the correct field is the world, not the Church. Jesus could have sat around the Temple courts letting people find Him if they wanted. He could have sent out His disciples to bring people back to His big "Temple Court Crusade."

Instead, He took the game to a different field.

Matthew 9:35-38 gives us one of the clearest summaries of Jesus' ministry:

> *"Jesus went through all the towns and villages, teaching in their synagogues, proclaiming the good news of the kingdom and healing every disease and sickness. When he saw the crowds, he had compassion on them, because they were harassed and helpless, like sheep without a shepherd. Then he said to his disciples, 'The harvest is plentiful but the workers are few. Ask the Lord of the harvest, therefore, to send out workers into his harvest field.'"*

Jesus went to where the people were. When He got there, He looked behind their masks and saw their individual pain: "*harassed and helpless, like sheep without a shepherd.*" Then, moved by compassion, He met their needs through preaching, teaching and healing.

A few verses later in Matthew 10 when Jesus sends out His disciples, He tells them to go find a neighborhood: *If you find a home that is receptive to the Kingdom, bring the peace of God to that home and by extension to that neighborhood.* The disciples were to undo the works of darkness and release the power of the Kingdom of light. They were to meet the needs of the neighborhood they were called to.

Once we begin to think multiplication, honor the Holy Spirit's power, and unleash ordinary disciples, we must plant them in a neighborhood they can serve. "Nurture" is a powerful word describing this work of church multiplication. A group of disciples senses a call to a specific neighborhood and begins to cultivate relationships there. (Neighborhoods can be a certain geographical neighborhood or a certain demographic like Harley Davidson riders, or the Anime crowd in the Los Angeles area, or a fraternity at Harvard.) As we nurture relationships, we begin to discover the needs of the neighborhood. Serving these needs then becomes the open door to bring the wisdom, power and compassion of Jesus to help heal the community.

My wife, Dr. Deb Walkemeyer, is responsible for starting the first community garden in Compton, California. It is quite a sight to see a lily white, middle-aged blonde standing in the middle of a large garden while the Bloods and Crips drive by, the prostitutes walk by, and the smell of weed (the burning kind) fills the air. But the neighborhood loves her. Now some of the neighbors are asking her, "When are you going to start a church here?"

Jesus instructs us that good deeds must be mixed with the Good News. Serving won't replace sharing. Jesus also warns us that some neighborhoods will reject the message, and we need to move on if they do. There is fertile soil elsewhere.

Nurturing a neighborhood happens when you find a neighborhood that grabs your heart. Actually, it twists your gut. In Matthew 9:36, Jesus saw the neighborhood and felt "compassion." The Greek word for "compassion" here literally means a "twisting of the intestines." You care so deeply that it grips your gut. This is the place church planting must flow from; without true compassion for the people in your church and around it, planting is only an impotent ministry strategy.

O-Organize around Jesus.

Level 5 churches build enduring structure organized around the person of Jesus.

Once a group of believers has been introduced to Jesus, they must be organized around Him. *Play thuno* is not a chaotic game without structure, leadership or accountability. The game has referees that call "fouls" and determine when something is out of bounds. The Church is not a holy democracy where every voice can claim leadership.

While the book of Acts introduces us to this unpredictable, spontaneous combustion of gospel fire, it also presents the reality of apostolic authority, church leadership, elders, deacons and doctrinal rulings. It is not an "every disciple do your own thing" and "every church for themselves" environment.

If movements are not organized, they become like rivers without banks—a mile wide and an inch deep. Give them a few months, and they evaporate. Soon, no one remembers they were even there. Nothing is left to multiply. You can't find generation one, two or three because they were radically organic but never organized.

A pastor friend told me about his city where another pastor there claims to have planted 50 churches. "The only problem is that I have never met anyone who is part of one of those churches," he said. "The church has had no discernible impact here." This church was so organic that they sprang up like a wildflower but lost their bloom within a month. They left nothing behind pointing others to God.

Multiplying churches should plan on growing mature enough and stable enough to reproduce. Giving birth shouldn't kill a mother church. "Mothers" may eventually die (no church has lived perpetually), but reproduction should not be the cause of death.

A limited amount of organizing develops structure and stability and is necessary to a church's durability. Without some structure, momentum never becomes movement. When we organize as a church, we create an identity as a body of believers instead of remaining as unconnected body parts with limited functionality. We shape a responsibility to one another and champion a mission unique to the body of people that God has brought together.

However, as vital as organization is, we enter into dangerous territory when the center begins to shift. This is a common fatal flaw of growing churches. As they increase in size, these churches begin to revolve around the personality or charisma of the pastor. People are drawn to his or her ministry style, giftedness, magnetism or authority. In the short run, this seems like a perk—"Come hear our pastor. Our pastor is hilarious, brilliant, cool, relevant, down to earth, hip, anointed." (Fill in the blank based on what crowd you run with.)

But in the long run, this pastor-centric focus is debilitating, threatened by the act of raising up other pastors and leaders: "What if the new leader is better than our pastor?" How can you call people to leave a church to plant if the pastor has been the organizing force of the church? My guess is you've probably heard the principle that *what you win people with, you win them to.* If you won them with a "wow" pastor, you won't get them to plant unless you have a bigger "wow" pastor.

Level 5 churches will usually be led by what business author Jim Collins defines as a "Level 5 leader" in his best-selling book *Good to Great*. These types of leaders, Collins writes, "build enduring greatness through a paradoxical blend of personal humility and professional will."[2] In other words, their need to be known doesn't obstruct their passion for the mission. Because it's not about them personally, they can freely empower others.

The same "shifting of center" happens if a church becomes organized around the building, or the children's ministry, or the incredible worship band or the church board, or the denominational label. Each of these areas can be helpful and healthy, but not if they're competing for the centerpiece of the church. The person and mission of Jesus must be the organizing center. While leadership is essential to the church, it cannot become the head of the church. That position is already occupied: *"For from him and through him and for him are all things. To him be the glory forever! Amen"* (Rom 11:36). If we blur the lines, we will quickly lose our path forward.

The Holiest Communion

For churches that choose to *play thuno*, Jesus is the bread and the wine. He is the food they eat and the life they drink. When they gather, it is to share in His life and to share His life with one another. When they depart, it is to take His life to their world. They take "communion" to the neighborhood.

One of the most meaningful communion services I ever participated in was at a pastors' conference I was leading in Portland, Oregon. After serving the bread, I passed out the cup to the pastors and asked them not to drink it. Instead, I told them that when they felt ready, to go to the busy intersection outside the church parking lot and pour out the cup as they prayed for the unsaved people driving by.

What transpired was powerful. As these pastors took the symbol of Christ's blood and poured it into the street, their hearts were broken for the lost. They recommitted themselves to pour out their lives by taking the church to the streets.

The church is not about our programs for Christ but about the person of Christ. When a church organizes around Him, Jesus is lifted up and draws people to Himself. This, my brothers and sisters, is the essence of church multiplication.

6

Game Stoppers

6 Deceptions that Derail Multiplication

We almost missed the game. Our church, Light & Life, had stopped the bleeding (Level 1), blazed upward past the plateau (Level 2) and now was experiencing the euphoria of church growth (Level 3). The harvest had been good. Our barns were full and overflowing.

So we thought to ourselves, *what shall we do?*

"Aw," we reasoned, "we'll tear down our barns and build bigger ones, and then we can take it easier and have an even bigger party."

But we felt the Lord saying to us, "Not an evil plan, but not the best one either. What if you gave a bunch of your grain to some of your servants and sent them out to plant their own farms?"

"But Lord, that is scarier, riskier, harder, and more humble than our plan."

"I know," He said. "My way usually is. It's your choice."

We chose to *play thuno*. Light & Life began planting churches (moving toward Level 4), and now we're trying to move towards being a true multiplying church (Level 5). In the United States, we've started 19 churches, and many more have sprung up in other nations. Far more people have been reached by multiple farms than by one bigger barn.

As we've already learned in the earlier chapters, the call to multiply weaves through the tapestry of Scripture. However, as we begin to read forward from Genesis 1, we hit some "game stoppers" capable of keeping leaders stuck in addition. If your church has moved forward to multiply, you've probably come up against some of these "deceptions" with the potential to derail multiplication. As you read about these game stoppers, ask the Holy Spirit which of these may be keeping your church from full engagement.

The Deception of Plan B

God's multiplication plan worked. Adam and Eve gladly answered God's call, and the earth began to fill with their offspring. But wickedness also multiplied, and God instituted a severe reduction plan called the flood. In the preparation for the flood, He was specific in His instructions to Noah to take "male and female" onto the ark—His view biased toward restoration.

After the flood, you may have thought that God would have tried "Plan B" since Plan A didn't work out that well. But notice His first words to Noah after they disembarked into a whole new world: "And God blessed Noah and his sons and said to them, 'Be fruitful and *multiply*, and fill the earth'" (Gen. 9:1).

Do those words sound familiar?

They are almost a verbatim repeat of God's directive to Adam and Eve in Genesis 1—Plan A repeated. If you and I were running the show, we'd have already gone to Plan B, C or D! Not God. He doesn't change the game. He simply invites in the new players for another game of *play thuno*.

As church leaders, we've wasted far too much time and money trying to engage a hip fad or celebrity-driven strategy to jumpstart the mission. Remember C.S. Lewis' words about the church: "I wish they'd remember that the charge to Peter was feed my sheep; not try experiments on my rats, or even, teach my performing dogs new tricks."[1] Until the church decides Plan A is the Master's exclusive plan for winning the world, we will keep losing the battle with culture.

My football coach used to sternly admonish our team, "'Fancy' doesn't win ball games. You must simply be better at the basics than the other team." We need to stop trying to invent the trick plays and instead get better at the basics—Plan A.

The Deception of Church Ishmaels

Abraham discovered the downside of departing from God's Plan A. When he was 75 years old, God promised him that he'd be "multiplied." But at age 85, still without a child, Abraham and Sarah cooked up their own plan B. In Genesis 16, Sarah's servant, Hagar, gives birth to Ishmael.

For the next 13 years, God is silent.

Finally, when Abraham is a ripe old 99 years of age, God breaks His silence and repeats Himself: "I will establish My covenant between Me and you, and I will multiply you exceedingly" (Gen. 17:2).

Abraham doesn't seem to get it. He reasons that at 99, there is *no physical way* he can produce this multiplication promise. So he makes another desperate plea for Ishmael to be the chosen church planter. I can just imagine what God thought, *Abraham, I've got you exactly where I want you—at the end of your own ability, without any substitute means of attaining My promise.* God goes on to promise that He will establish His everlasting covenant through Isaac (Gen. 17:19).

One of the dominant deceptions of the church has been our dependency upon our own strategies and self-effort to bring about the promises of God. Stepping over the fine line between co-laboring with God and drawing up our own blueprints often gives birth to our own church "Ishmaels." Cheating on God by loving and trusting ourselves always leads to some deformity in what our strategies generate.

For sever years, our church talked about multiplying, but nothing happened. We felt God had promised we would multiply, but after almost a decade we were still barren. So my mind started working overtime on how to fix us up with another suitor. We found a dying church that owned a run-down building and sent a pastoral couple to it, along with a few other naïve guinea pigs. We proudly declared we had done it; we had planted a church. Surely this was the start of something glorious.

After only a few months, it was obvious we had given birth to "Ishmael." It became a wild situation that ended up poorly for nearly everyone involved. I had fallen into the deception of "substitutionary attainment." I repented, and we began to listen more carefully and patiently for God's plan instead of our human strategy.

Abraham eventually learned to *play thuno* God's way and became the father of multitudes, but it was through faith and obedience, not his self-directed efforts. The church is not a secular corporation, and multiplication is not a business strategy to be implemented. Any approach that's not bathed in prayer, borne by faith, and birthed by the Spirit will ultimately fail.

The Deception of American Idols

The next time we see this multiplication theme is in Genesis 22. Abraham now has his promised son Isaac, his golden child. No doubt Abraham and Isaac have developed a close relationship as Isaac has grown. It's not overly imaginative to picture Abraham loving Isaac more dearly the more Isaac grew.

Shockingly, there comes a point in time when God asks Abraham to sacrifice his only true son—the son He repeatedly promised to give Abraham. (The Jewish historian, Josephus, states that Isaac was 25 years old when Genesis 22 occurs on Mount Moriah.[2]) I can't fathom the interior debate that must have raged in Abraham's mind. Nevertheless, in an act of faith and obedience he lays his cherished son on the sacrificial wood. Of course we know that at the last moment, God provides the substitutionary lamb and Isaac is spared.

But have you ever focused on God's response to Abraham's sacrifice?

> *"… By Myself I have sworn, declares the LORD, because you have done this thing and have not withheld your son, your only son, indeed I will greatly bless you, and I will greatly multiply your seed as the stars of the heavens and as the sand which is on the seashore; and your seed shall possess the gate of their enemies"* (Gen. 22:16-17, NASB).

It is as if God says, "Abraham, since you were willing to lay down the very thing you prayed for, worked for, loved, adored, found such joy in, had such great expectations for … therefore, I am going to fulfill My promise of multiplication." In this context, I suggest the "pre-altar Isaac" can illustrate "addition," while the" post-altar Isaac" could represent "multiplication."

I doubt you'll argue that the American Church is in love with "church growth," in love with becoming or being a "Level 3" church. Sometimes it seems we have an idol of "addition." As with Isaac's birth, church growth brings us great pleasure, and we celebrate its arrival. Addition is indeed a huge blessing, a gift from God, a reason to rejoice, and frankly it's much better than the alternative of subtraction. Ongoing addition is essential to multiplication.

But when the gift of God becomes an idol, compromising your worship of Him and stealing some of your affection for Him, then get ready! A Mount Moriah showdown is coming. When the gift of addition begins to threaten the promise of multiplication, it starts to become a curse.

In their book, *Becoming a Level 5 Multiplying Church*, Todd Wilson and Dave Ferguson point out that the financial and leadership resources needed to feed the beast in Level 3 (addition) are the same resources needed to fuel multiplication in Levels 4 (reproducing) and 5 (multiplying). "When this tyranny of the *or* emerges," they write, "addition growth usually wins out over multiplication."[3]

Addition is fantastic when it's a catalyst for multiplication. But when addition becomes an object of our affection rather than a source through which multiplication will flow, it has become an American Church idol.

To state it squarely, you can't *play thuno* if you have an idol of addition.

The Deception of 'When & Then'

Fast forward from Abraham to Exodus 1. The children of Israel are in Egypt under less than ideal conditions. Racism develops and unleashes its poison into the minds of the Egyptian leaders. Slavery ensues. The Israelites are groaning under the pressures of this discrimination. They long to live in a different country. They dream of Canaan's land.

It was a time when it would have been easy to say, "Let's wait until times improve to bear children. Why have a baby when our identity and culture are under such heavy attack? It's time to withdraw, circle our proverbial wagons and protect what we have. *When* life gets easier, *when* circumstances are more conducive, *then* we will have our children. This is a serious season, now is not the time to multiply!"

Instead, something amazing happened that caused the culture and the powers around them to take notice and tremble. We read of it in Exodus 1:12: "*But the more they were oppressed, the more they multiplied and spread; so the Egyptians came to dread the Israelites.*"

Oppression led to multiplication. Times were tough, but they decided to *play thuno*! The Israelites weren't waiting for "when and then." They were living out God's promises to them despite the culture around them.

Here's my concern with the Church in America: We are waiting for a time that will never come. We are looking for an idyllic moment when all systems are go…*When* we have all the seats full, money in the bank, a bench full of leaders, a unanimous board vote, no resistance from the city or culture around us, the perfect building available, etc., *then* we will multiply.

Remember my rabbits I raised? They never waited for the mood music and candlelit dinner. They were born to multiply, and that's what they did regardless of the size of their pen or the food in their bowl. Any obstacles in their current situation could not stop their God-given DNA and their personal priority.

Look at the past 100 years of the Church in China. In the face of persecution, the Chinese Church has multiplied. Throughout history, persecution has often become the necessary ignition for multiplication.

In my opinion, there are two foundational reasons for this miracle of multiplication under persecution. First, persecution strips the Church of its optional accessories and focuses it on the empowered essentials. While screens, lights, amplification, media, Disneyland children areas, food courts and hip worship bands offer pizazz that attracts people to church, they can also dilute the focus on the life-giving basics— multiplicative disciple making and the reproduction of new churches. During persecution, smaller gatherings that multiply rapidly become a vital necessity instead of an optional strategy.

Second, persecution begets humility and dependency. I am a fan of comfortable seats in a church building However, if you take away the seats, you're left with no alternative but to sit on the floor and pray your heart out for revival. This is what my Ethiopian village friends do, and their mud hut churches are overflowing and reproducing rapidly. Humility attracts God's blessing and power. It also avoids the arrogance that addition can easily breed. Multiplication with decentralized leadership makes it difficult to become a celebrity.

The "here and now" instead of "when and then" mindset births a Level 5 church. Waiting for your church's weather to change produces debilitating procrastination. But when you see multiplication as the call of every church all the time, it becomes an "all season" priority.

The Deception of Clutching

When my daughter, Lindsey, was nearing two years of age, she had the strongest grip I've ever seen in any child and most adults. Once she grabbed hold of something she wanted, you needed a chisel to pry her tiny fingers loose. Regardless of what I said or did, Lindsey was determined to hang on to what she had.

I soon discovered a more effective means of dealing with her clutching problem. If I held in front of her something she wanted more than what she currently had, then she easily surrendered whatever object she was clenching. The only snafu to my approach was locating something she fancied more. If I could have crawled inside her little head, I believe I would have found a big wad of fear behind Lindsey's iron fist: *I've got this. I like this. If I give it up, I won't get anything else.*

In our ministry lives, it's not usually our idolatry or carnality that causes our clutching but rather our fear, insecurity in God's math, our job security or our identity security. *If I let go, God may not give me something better.* Instead, we may end up empty-handed. Fear will always confine us to the sidelines of *play thuno.*

In 2 Kings chapter 4, we catch up with another example of multiplication. This time, it's more immediate and personal. One of Elisha's associate pastors has died, leaving behind a wife and two boys with no life insurance or pension plan. The situation goes from bad to worse when the landlord sends his henchmen over to draft the widow's two boys as slaves.

The widow begs Elisha for help, and Elisha asks the right question.

"What do you already have?"

"Nothing except a small jar of oil," the widow replies.

And then Elisha basically says, "A small jar of oil is enough to see multiplication happen *if* you will open your hand to release what you have. *If* you will trust our God to do His math, you will have plenty. *If* you will pour it out in faith, He will keep it flowing."

The widow immediately sends her sons door-to-door soliciting empty jars, and they collect as many as possible. Then she starts pouring … and pouring ... and pouring. When she fills every jar to the brim, she asks, "Are there any more?" Would she have asked this if her own original jar was unfilled? No! Her original jar was still filled to the brim. Lesson: It's easy to pour out when you know there's more.

So often I have stopped God's flow because of my fear, my doubt, my clutching. I have hindered God's miracles because I felt what I had was too small. This widow had only a small jar of oil. Your church doesn't have to be a certain size to multiply and become a Level 5 example of multiplication. It's not the size of the jar; it's the openness of our hand and the power of the Spirit that counts.

The Deception of Inactive Intentions

A similar miracle to the widow's happens in Jesus' ministry (Mark 6). A megachurch crowd has gathered to hear the carpenter teach about the Kingdom He is building. As evening approaches, the roar of their rumbling stomachs compete with the carpenter's message. The disciples had a plan and suggested it to Jesus: "Call a timeout so the folks can go buy some grub for themselves" (Mark 6:36).

But Jesus had a different idea. "Why don't you give them something to eat?" He asked them.

One of the disciples, probably Judas or Matthew, did some quick math and basically asked, "Are you serious? We are talking six months of paychecks to even buy appetizers for a group this size!" Jesus replied, "Go see what you've got to work with."

When the disciples returned with five loaves of bread and two fish, Jesus didn't say, "Well that isn't enough." Instead, He remarked, "Okay, then have them sit down in groups of a hundred." Then He took the picnic basket, lifted it to Heaven, and prayed something like, "God is great, God is good and we thank Him for this food."

Next, He broke off half of a loaf, grabbed the few pieces of fish and gave it all to each of the disciples to distribute. Right at that moment was the hinge point of the miracle. They were facing groups of hundreds of people with only half a loaf of bread in their baskets. Would the disciples turn their intentions into actions? Would they put commitment to their compassion? Would they step out to make their faith tangible and taste-able?

Aren't you curious when the multiplication of the loaves and fish actually occurred? Was it in Jesus' blessing? Then a huge stack of bread would have suddenly piled up in front of Jesus. Was it in the actual act of breaking the bread? Then Jesus would have stood there for four or more hours simply breaking enough bread for 8,000 people. Scripture doesn't point to either of these times.

Instead, the miracle appears to happen in the act of distribution. As each disciple reaches into his basket, another loaf appears. Twelve disciples handing out already broken loaves could have completed the job in a little over an hour.

Several years ago, I was helping a missionary organize a dinner for a small village in a remote part of the world. We expected 50 people at the most to attend. However, as the time drew closer, more than 300 people had arrived. Now we were concerned about hostilities breaking out in the crowd as some would eat but most would not. At a loss for how to remedy the situation, we quieted the crowd, gave thanks for the food and asked God for His multiplication miracle to occur. We thought perhaps a lost food truck would suddenly drive up to the scene. But nothing happened.

So we decided to serve what we had to whom we could. As we started to serve the jostling crowd, we began to sense something strange. The bowls we were serving from always had two or three more helpings. We didn't see it happen, but it did. Would it surprise you if I told you we sent leftovers home with people?

Here's the point: Multiplication happens during distribution—not in the dreaming, the planning, the praying, the feeling, the intending. It is in the doing, during the action. You don't *play thuno* by holding on to your cards. You give them away.

When mother churches only talk, plan, dream and scheme about multiplication, they fail to see the miracles of God's provision. However as they turn intentions into actions, stumble forward, and give away what they have, the miracles of multiplication begin.

Having led our church to daughter multiple churches, I have watched this happen in various ways. I have seen God multiply dollars, leaders, open doors, connections, sound systems, chairs, political favor and facilities. But God never blessed our *intentions*, only our *actions*.

I remember one church plant that searched without success for a facility. They felt convicted that God would meet them in the doing, not the dreaming. So they announced their launch date with no facility secured yet. (Not a good church-planting plan, to be sure.) On the invitations, they printed something like, "Pray with us for the location. We'll let you know as soon as we know!" Within the next three weeks, three facilities had been offered to them. Their intentions became actions and in the distribution, multiplication happened.

Jesus said, "You will know the truth and the truth will set you free" (John 8:32). I've found that promise to be true, but if I'm being honest, often the truth first cuts me open for heart surgery. As a church leader,

I want the truth—the truth about my leadership, the truth about our church, the truth about the gospel mission in my corner of the world.

So one of my most pressing prayers simply says, "Lord, tell me the truth about me." Or, "Lord, tell me the truth about our church." I ask Him, "Search us and show us what is hindering us from having a greater impact upon the world around us. What is stopping us from becoming a multiplication movement?"

When you honestly and humbly pray this prayer, the Spirit will be faithful to reveal what deceptive "game stopper" is keeping you from multiplying your church.

7

Winning Moves

21 Leadership Essentials for Multiplication

Although we aren't Pentecostal, the church I lead is enthusiastic. During worship, I often "dance" around in my limited front seat floor space. My "dancing" is the cause of ceaseless good-natured ribbing, especially because our multiethnic church is populated by agile dancers. I've often playfully responded, "Give me a break, white men can't jump or dance!"

I remember telling one of our members, "I can't dance, but I have fun!" He quickly corrected me, "Pastor, you *can* dance, you just have to learn the steps. I can teach you the moves. You might not win 'Dancing With the Stars' but you can dance!"

I hope by now you realize that every Jesus-centered church can dance! Multiplication is not reserved for a select, elite group, exclusive to certain sizes or styles of church. Your church can win at the game of *play thuno*, but you have to learn and practice the right moves. Certain behavioral characteristics and actions result in multiplication. It's up to us to learn and practice each one.

First, allow me to offer my definition of "winning" at multiplication. In this "game," we aren't competing against anyone except the evil one and the kingdom of darkness. We are playing for "eternal souls." The "win" is in reaching the harvest field that God has called your church to, and being the church you were created to be in your specific context.

Winning is becoming a church that's structured around the Kingdom priority of multiplication, allowing for continual reproduction through the church *and* through her offspring to the point that the fourth generation church is actively reproducing. In a winning church, a culture of giving birth within the church's first 36 months permeates each of the daughter generations. This is the goal line in *play thuno*.

How do we journey there? What steps will we need to take? What moves can we make to birth a multiplication movement from our existing church?

High Priority Moves

1. Sold-out senior leadership: If a church's senior leader is not sold out to the idea of Level 5 multiplication, there is near zero possibility of the church moving forward. The leader must change or you must change who's leading. Leaders who are deeply convinced of the biblical call to multiply will be convincing to others. They must commit to trading in their "church growth" passion (addition) for a "Kingdom growth" passion (multiplication).

This was the single most difficult move for me. The American Church culture rewards addition, and I must die daily to its siren call on my ego. I had to fully believe that the size of my church did not define the reach of my church.

I had to start to see our church as an aspen instead of a redwood.

Let me explain. Redwoods are the tallest trees in the world, reaching an average height of 379 feet. Aspens usually grow to only 70 feet—only one fifth the height of a redwood. But aspens grow in a different way. The aspen sends out roots that spring up into new trees. These new trees can grow as far as 130 feet from the first aspen. After only a few years, you can find an entire grove or colony of aspens that have sprung up from a single aspen tree.

At Light & Life, our original church has continued to grow through addition, but we keep giving people away in church plants. Sometimes we send out large numbers of our people, which causes our church attendance numbers to go up and down. But our "aspen grove" is now 10 times larger, and these other aspens are now producing their own new colonies of trees. A forest is growing. As we committed to multiplication, we began to measure our impact by the quality of the disciples we were making and the launch of multiplying churches. At one time, I wanted a redwood church over an aspen. Now, when I picture our church five or 10 years from now, I picture an aspen grove.

Question: How deeply do you/your church's senior leader embrace the value of multiplication? Is that belief consistently evident through your leadership behavior and your church's practices?

2. Consistent and compelling communication: To change a culture, you must first change the values. Granted, this is difficult. It begins by influencing the influencers with the *why* for the change. Tap into the motivation for the change and tie it to the values your church/ leadership team already shares (such as reaching the lost with the gospel).

Through relational conversations, we must explain the theological underpinnings and sociological realities of Level 5 thinking. (Give them the book *Becoming a Level 5 Multiplying Church* to read.) Staff and influencers need to buy into multiplication to the point that they can give an elevator speech detailing the rationale and emotions for this change in the church's culture—carrying the conversation to the whole church.

Question: How clear and compelling is your "elevator speech" explaining the rationale for moving towards Level 5? What percentage of the leaders and members in your church can give the speech?

3. Intercession: If our spiritual enemy understands the power of multiplication, then doesn't it follow that he will level his most formidable spiritual weaponry against it? Consequently, our counter-attack is our air attack. We send in the prayer warriors like B-52 bombers ahead of our ground troops to remove the spiritual ambushes against us.

When Light & Life committed to moving from Level 3 to Level 4, we knew there would be intense spiritual resistance. So we marshaled various forms of prayer coverage. We went to the highest point of the city and prayed. We walked areas where churches would be planted and prayed. We fasted and prayed. We had all-night prayer meetings. We launched special prayer teams focused largely on church planting. I'm convinced these moves were major factors in our ability to transition our church.

Question: What level of intercessory prayer—especially focused on multiplication—is currently happening in your church?

4. Teaching: To change the multiplication culture of our church, we need to identify and maximize our primary delivery points for teaching. Our weekend messages and small group curriculum give us opportunities to imbed multiplication concepts into our church's culture through in-depth Bible teaching.

Every year, we spend the first four to five Sundays teaching through the values driving the decisions we make to multiply. Throughout the year, we revisit this subject in a variety of ways, reminding our church that we are wonderfully different than other churches.

Question: To what degree do your church's public and small group teaching explain and support the various concepts of multiplication thinking? How often do you reference multiplication in your teaching?

5. Strategy: Simon Sinek's best-selling book, *Start With Why*, underscores the priority of "why" over "how" and "what." Each time I read it, I cheer. You see, I'm a great "why" guy– strong in passion and weak on plans. We misread Sinek, however, if we think we can ignore the strategy of "how." We must move beyond convictions to systems. Without a "how," our "why" remains a disembodied dream.

The first poster I remember seeing in a pastor's office read, "If you fail to plan, you better plan to fail." I was this pastor's student intern for the semester. He saw me looking at the poster and asked me, "So what's our plan to raise more money for missions?" I hesitantly answered, "Pray?" He beamed, "Great answer! What's step two of our plan?"

Until we have a strategy for multiplication, we aren't serious about multiplication. The best strategy is the one we will actually use. Too many strategies sit in notebooks on shelves collecting dust. Learn about multiplication, select a model, put it into practice, and adjust it as you go.

Question: How clearly thought through and written out is your multiplication strategy?

6. Discipleship: We have countless definitions for discipleship, however I believe a person is considered discipled when she can lead another person to Christ and adequately train her to be a disciple maker. In most cultures, physical maturity has historically been marked by the ability to reproduce. Spiritual maturity should be similar.

Multiplication is not an isolated approach to expanding the Church; it is an outgrowth of disciple making. If our people aren't multiplying themselves through disciple making, then moving towards multiplication is really just imposing another program on people. Multiplying churches begin with disciples multiplying disciples.

Question: To what degree is your church actively engaged in discipleship that makes disciples?

7. Small Groups: One of our leaders started a small group with no intention of becoming a church planter. He had a vision, however, for the small group to be atypical—they would serve their community, reach the lost, challenge one another towards full deployment of their gifts, and start new groups. In 12 months, this leader was in my office talking to me about starting a church. Within another six months, he and his network launched a powerful new church.

Small groups are either the dynamic breeding grounds for new churches or the tranquil gathering place for saints to relax into self-affirming fellowship. As leaders, it's up to us to repurpose our small groups around a multiplication agenda where saints are actively discovering their gifts through using them; interceding together for the harvest fields; equipping one another to "go"; serving on mission together; and planning the next group they'll start within the year.

Question: To what degree are your small groups thinking of multiplying themselves? In what ways are they contributing to the launch of new churches?

8. Financials: Jesus' words in Matthew 6:21 are brilliant: "Where your treasure is, there will your heart be also." In that simple line, He revealed the inner workings of the human heart. Getting your heart and mind into multiplication mode begins with putting your money there.

Practically, multiplication requires us to establish a budget that prioritizes funding for it (a tithe of 10 percent of annual revenues)—before the first planting team is even in view.

For three years, Light & Life budgeted for church planting by putting money in a special fund each month. We could have used that money on several urgent needs and some really cool desires, but we refused to touch that church-planting treasure chest. As the treasure chest grew, so did our passion to plant a church.

Question: To what degree does your budget demonstrate your church's commitment to multiplication? What level of sacrificial investment have you, personally, made in that direction?

9. Metrics: What you treasure, you measure. What you expect, you inspect. What you cherish, you chart. Every leader and every church has an internal scoreboard that is constantly adding or subtracting points. Each scoreboard is particular to that leader or church based upon their values and vision.

Our challenge comes in building a scoreboard that measures what truly matters most. Our scoreboards tend to be built around the quick, easy, visible "points." At the onset, multiplication is slow while addition is rapid and attractive. In our church, Kingdom measurements are a combination of what we call "stats and stories." We ask, "What are the numbers?" *and* "What are the names?" "What are the facts?" *and* "Who are the faces?" As we focus our scoreboards on multiplication values (disciple makers, reproductive small groups, church plants that plant churches, etc.), we acquire a much more accurate view of our Kingdom impact.

Question: Is your internal scoreboard aligned with multiplication values and vision? What about the scoreboards of leaders on your team?

10. Stories: The ancient practice of sitting around a campfire telling stories of courage demonstrated and shaped the values of the tribe. Storytelling is the glue holding your tribe together—capturing, highlighting and retelling stories of disciples who are making disciples; small groups starting small groups; or especially of new churches being planted.

If we hope to instill multiplication, our churches must tell the right stories, tell them well and repeat them often. We have to position multiplication stories as headlines at services and save the biggest headlines to honor church plants that plant another church.

Question: What stories are shaping your church and its values?

11. Farm team: Mark was a super-star dairy salesman. When he came to Light & Life, I asked him, "Have you ever considered pointing your 'people skills' towards full-time ministry?"

He basically replied, "I'm happy selling milk and making lots of money."

I asked, "Would you help us plant our next church, and would you pray about your future?"

He agreed. Today Mark pastors a vibrant church.

I'm convinced there are thousands of "Marks" out there—leaders waiting to be discovered, to be asked, to be developed, They simply need to get near contagious, healthy leaders who have an empowering, multiplication mindset and will invite them to listen for God's direction in their lives.

All churches need a farm team that causes us to habitually ask, "Who's on our bench ready to become a starter?" As leaders, part of our call is to continually scout both inside and outside the church for new leaders, even initiating an intern program.

Question: Do you have a developed system for empowering upcoming leaders into positions where they can multiply for the Kingdom?

12. Staffing: In a staff configured around multiplication, each "in-house" staff member must see his primary role as "cloning" himself. For example, the children pastor's first job is not to run the program for kids but to raise up a kids minister who can go with the next church plant.

In a multiplication culture, every staff member is "fair game" for God to call to planting. At Light & Life, we have often hired people for a short-term period for the express purpose of planting them in a new church. We also say to our "in-house" staff, "It's okay if you're next!" We hire a minimum of one church planter for every two in-house church ministers.

Question: To what degree is your staff serving the church's multiplication vision? Do you have positions (interns, volunteer staff, staff) preparing to be sent?

13. Membership: Are your membership or partnership classes designed around the priority of multiplication? Rather than seeing the commitment of membership as a lifelong vow to the mother church, reframe and repurpose it as a commitment to the mission of the church.

Membership classes are excellent opportunities for sharing the primary stories defining your tribe. Declare the dream that God has given your church. Don't sugarcoat the difference between your church and the typical American church. We call members to surrender their lives to the harvest values our church lives by and from the outset, communicate,

"Some of you will stay, but eventually most of you will go to start new works. We are a 'river' church, and we give our best away."

Question: How well does your membership/partnership process serve the multiplication value of your church? How well do your members understand your church's priority on planting?

14. Gift development: Jerry was one of our best ushers, and in my mind that's where he was stuck: *Thank you, Jesus, for a solid usher who gets to use his gifts for your glory!* Then one day, Jerry said he was going with one of our church plants. Next thing I knew, Jerry was practically running the whole church—leading prayer meetings, preaching, leading servant teams, etc. What happened? Our church planter invested in him, discovered his gifts, trusted him with significant ministry and cheered him forward. I was rightly humbled as I watched this transformation.

Multiplication requires a much higher belief in the capabilities and gifts of believers. Remember that they are potential world changers, led by the Spirit. People can discern when someone believes in and trusts them with greater responsibility. Faith in ordinary people to do the unexpected fuels multiplication movements. If God endows individuals with strengths and abilities at creation, then He indwells them with His Spirit at salvation, and then imparts spiritual gifts to them. We have every reason to expect great things from "normal" disciples.

Leverage ongoing classes, seminars and training to come alongside church members and help them identify and develop their strengths, spiritual gifts and talents toward multiplication. Serving within the church becomes the training ground, not the endgame, for pioneering new works.

Question: To what degree does your "average" member know, appreciate and use his or her strengths, gifts and talents towards multiplication?

15. Facilities: Our 39 parking spots in our urban setting have been a bane and a blessing. They have forced us into seasons of chronological gymnastics as we've bent over backward to create service times to accommodate everyone. On the other hand, that limited number of spaces has helped keep our foot on the pedal of church planting. Sometimes I wonder if we would have pursued church planting so aggressively if we had 500 spaces.

I fully believe that unless the Church in America releases its affair with buildings, we may never see a multiplication movement. Mortgage debt is undermining many churches that would love to jump into church planting but can't financially afford to send attendees out the door. Their generosity is hobbled by their indebtedness on their buildings. Until pastors are far more interested in building the Church with "living stones," than with bricks and mortar, we will block God's vision for pervasive church planting. Practically, this means committing to planting churches before acquiring newer, more, or better facilities. The church is built around the people and the mission instead of the building.

Facilities are wonderful tools when purposed towards multiplication. But when built around addition, they become impediments to the better vision.

Question: To what degree are your current facilities (and your planned facilities) keeping you from multiplying? To what degree are your multiplication dreams unhindered by your mortgage debt?

16. Mission statement: People love hooks—short sayings packed with meaning and passion. Hooks help me recall our calling. Mission statements can be hooks aligning your people to the values.

Our goal at Light & Life is to ensure that anyone who has been attending our church for two months or more can recite the simplified version of our mission statement: Reach, Teach, Mend, Send! Those four words define so much about our values and calling. It's a cheer we use often. Each time we do, people are reminded that we exist to *send*. Of course, it also works in reverse. Anyone who visits our church quickly learns what we're about. So if they don't embrace that mission, they can depart quickly and gracefully.

Question: Do you have a memorable mission statement declaring your priority on sending, planting, or multiplication? Can 90 percent of your current attendees share it?

17. Vision clarity: A leader's job is to define reality, create values, cast vision and serve the values and vision of the church by recruiting others to join them in the journey. Someone has said, "We usually overestimate what we can do in one year and underestimate what we can do in 10." This is certainly the case if you don't comprehend the power of multiplication.

For example, simple math shows us that a congregation with only three healthy small groups multiplying themselves just once every year can multiply to 3,072 small groups in 10 years. To be honest, I've never seen that math work in a real church setting, but even if you hit 30 percent of that number, there would be nearly 1,000 small groups. As leaders, it's our responsibility to lift our church's eyes above addition to the amazing vision of multiplication.

Practically, that means casting a one-, five-, 10- and 40-year vision centered on multiplication. Help people envision the immediate, the short-term, the mid-range and the generational future by painting the picture for them and forecasting possible numbers. Boggle their minds and stir their hearts with the generational possibilities of multiplication compared to addition.

Question: How clear and compelling is the vision I have cast for our church? Do our church leaders own that vision? Does our church?

18. Visual support: Our church logo is designed to convey the value of multiplication. Our defining image is "The River" church. When people ask, "What's a river church?" our people are ready with their elevator speech of what it is and why it's important. (Read our story in the FREE eBook *Flow: Unleashing a River of Multiplication in Your Church, City and World*.)[1]

Pictures and symbols carry meaning and create culture with a profound effectiveness. Decorate with your multiplication mission in mind. For example, use high-quality pictures of church planters, new congregations, and pastors baptizing in new areas of the city. Design your church logo with your multiplication values embedded into it.

Question: To what degree do your visuals (in your church, online, and in the community) tell your church's story and communicate your multiplication vision?

19. Network: One of God's gifts to the Church in the last decade has been the proliferation of church-planting networks that exist to expedite the planting of healthy and effective gospel-centered churches. Exponential has been a pioneer in this regard. Though they don't plant churches like networks such as ARC and The Orchard Group, they are currently delivering a plethora of resources that pastors and leaders can access.

Scripture is clear in Proverbs 24:6: *"Surely you need guidance to wage war, and victory is won through many advisers."* Church planting is spiritual warfare of the most intense kind. Don't be foolish. Seek out and equip yourself and your church with all the guidance, support, and resources that God has made available. Don't travel this road alone. Put coaches and accountability into place. This is Kingdom work requiring the encouragement, prayers and wisdom of people and organizations focused on multiplication.

Question: Are you an active part of one or more healthy networks of church planters/coaches?

20. Multi-Everything: Diversity is a good friend of multiplication because multiplication exists and thrives within a cohesive culture interwoven with diversity, not through uniformity. I counsel young church planters, "Champion multi-ethnic, multi-generational, multi-economic, multi-worship styles, multi-size, multi-missional—multi-everything."

In the early days of Light & Life, we were a handful of Anglos in a neighborhood that looked like the United Nations. God answered our prayer of, "Lord help us look like our neighborhood," and we began to reach people from various races. Over the years, this reality has aided our church planting in profound ways. Although we stress that all of our church plants be multi-ethnic, each one of them leaves with a certain flavor. We have sent out Cambodian, Samoan, African-American, Chilean, Mexican, Filipino, Guatemalan, Nigerian, Irish and even Anglo church-planting pastors. This diversity gives us the opportunity to plant more broadly and rapidly than most homogeneous churches.

Question: To what degree does your church reflect the diversity in your church-planting region?

21. City-/region-focused: Ask yourself, *how would 20 more of our kind of church change the 20-minute radius I live in?* More than 80 percent of Americans live in urban areas with dense populations. In our case at Light & Life, our 20-minute radius encompasses roughly 1.5 million people. There is clearly room for 20 (or even 1,000) more of our brand of churches.

When you define an area, you begin to pray, dream and plan differently. Your heart begins to be burdened in a unique way. Just as Jesus wept over Jerusalem, you start to see your city through the eyes of a shepherd of your city, as well as your church.

The most profound impact you can make as a church planter is to gain a vision for a defined area in your city and begin to dream of the gospel impact that multiple churches of various sizes and styles could have on the people in that area. Share that vision with your church and begin to serve the needs in that place. Instead of building a bigger church, build a movement of churches to reach this area that you and your church have been dreaming about, praying for and serving.

Question: Does a defined area in your city pull at your heart, a place where you would love to see multiple vibrant churches?

These 21 important moves can help you learn the multiplication "dance." Although this list is by no means exhaustive, it might seem exhausting to you. Resist that feeling. Moving towards becoming a Level 5 multiplying church is a journey. What I've provided is simply a bit of a map to help you chart your course. Rest assured, you are not alone on this trip. The Spirit of God cares far more than you do about moving your church to multiply.

Below is an exercise to help you evaluate how far you are into this journey (remember this is a rough estimate):

1. Consider each of the 21 questions above and how they apply to your church.
2. Now assign your church a rating on a scale of 1 to 10 points for each question.

    1 = "nearly non-existent in our church"
    10 = "as much as reasonably possible"

3. Add up your total points and use the following rating scale:

160 to 210	Your church is structured around multiplication and is seeing it happen.
120 to 159	You're experiencing some of the thrill of multiplication and want more.
100 to 119	You're beginning to practice some of the essentials of multiplication.
70 to 99	You're understanding some of the essentials of multiplication.
0 to 69	You're just beginning to consider the idea of multiplication.

If you chose to score your church (and did it honestly), my guess is your rating may be a little disheartening. Mine was. I was convicted—but more convinced than ever—that moving towards Level 5 is God's desire for His church. Resist discouragement. The encourager, the Holy Spirit, is speaking power and possibility into your spirit, even in this moment.

The Church belongs to Jesus. He has promised to build it. He is the multiplier. What He did with the loaves and fishes, the disciples, and the churches in the book of Acts, He can do in your church. Your multiplication potential is as powerful and as miraculous as God's own ability.

Feed your spirit with the promise that God makes to you in Ephesians 3:20-21:

> *Now to him who is able to do immeasurably more than all we ask or imagine, according to his power that is at work within us, to him be glory in the church and in Christ Jesus throughout all generations, for ever and ever! Amen."*

EPILOGUE

The Post-Game

Not all churches will embrace multiplication. Most may sit in the stands and watch. But Kingdom-minded churches, harvest-focused churches, high-impact churches and generationally aware churches will awaken to a yearning to *play thuno.*

Vital churches cannot live in the stale air of Level 2 (survival), or the good air of Level 3 (addition), or even the fresh air of Level 4 (reproduction). They crave the pure oxygen of Level 5 (multiplication). These churches realize they're in a life-or-death battle with principalities and powers bent on destroying as many as possible. This is a daily battle for the eternal souls of people. All models of church life must be submitted to the one criterion that matters most: "How can we introduce the most people to a vital, saving relationship with Jesus?" The answer to that question *must* inform and shape your church's values, structures, methods, budgets and leadership. The answer to that question is clear: Structuring a church for multiplication has exponentially the greatest Kingdom potential.

"Level 5" churches will be the most impactful churches on earth. Whatever fears, tensions and excuses you bring to the playing field, rise above them and join the game for the sake of a Kingdom ruled by a Creator who loves the people He has created.

The church I serve as lead pastor is large but not a megachurch. Although I have served there for 25 years, I truly believe our most significant impact is just beginning. We used to be an "adding" church (Level 3) that awakened to being a "reproducing" church (Level 4). But now we are committed to becoming a life-giving, eternity-altering, "multiplying" church (Level 5).

Already an amazing phenomenon is occurring. In the few months since we started directing our prayers and conversations towards this multiplication shift, some of our daughter churches have announced they are "pregnant!" They will soon be planting other churches. We have a few "grandchildren" on the way. But I'm already thinking of and praying for "great-grandchildren." From now on, I will do my best to teach our "kids" and "grandkids" *to play thuno.*

When the church in America aggressively pursues "Level 5," the message of Christ will sweep this nation. This is the "game" we were created for.

May we all play it well for the glory of God!

ENDNOTES

Introduction // Discovering the Game

1. Todd Wilson and Dave Ferguson, *Becoming a Level 5 Multiplying Church Field Guide* (Exponential Resources, 2015)

Chapter 1 // Playing the Game

1. Ed Stetzer, "5 Reasons Established Churches Should Plant Churches," *Christianity Today*, 2014

2. Ibid

3. David T. Olson, *The American Church in Crisis: Groundbreaking Research Based on a National Database of Over 200,000 Churches* (Zondervan, 2008)

Chapter 2 // The Priority of the Game

1. http://acrlog.org/wp-content/uploads/2014/01/learningpyramid5.jpg

2. Christian Schwarz and Christopher Schalk, *Implementation Guide to Natural Church Development* (ChurchSmart Resources, 1998)

Chapter 3 // First Editions

1. *http://www.forbes.com/sites/kevinkruse/2013/04/09/what-is-leadership/#61571a30713e*

2. Oswald Chambers, *My Utmost for His Highest* (Oswald Chambers Publications Association, Ltd., 1935)

Chapter 5 // Strategies of the the Game

1. http://sourcesofinsight.com/simplicity-quotes/

2. Jim Collins, *Good to Great and the Social Sector: A Monograph to Accompany Good to Great* (HarperCollins Publishers 2005), 12.

Chapter 6 // Game Stoppers

1. C.S. Lewis, *The Joyful Christian* (Scribner, Touchstone, 1996)

2. http://biblehub.com/commentaries/genesis/22-1.htm

3. Todd Wilson and Dave Ferguson, *Becoming a Level 5 Multiplying Church Field Guide* (Exponential Resources, 2015)

Chapter 7 // Winning Moves

1. Larry Walkemeyer, *Flow: Unleashing a River of Multiplication in Your Church, City and World* (Exponential Resources, 2014)

ABOUT
LARRY WALKEMEYER

LARRY WALKEMEYER serves as the Lead Pastor of Light & Life Christian Fellowship in Long Beach, California. Starting with a handful of committed "white folks," the church has grown into a large multi-ethnic church, transforming its tough urban neighborhood. A priority on local and global church planting has led to the start of twenty-two churches nationally and dozens in Ethiopia, Philippines, and Indonesia.

As Director of Equipping and Spiritual Engagement for Exponential, Larry seeks to influence the church of Jesus toward multiplication. Holding a doctorate in church leadership and as the author of eight books (five for Exponential), Larry speaks and consults frequently. Azusa Pacific University has recognized Larry with the Centennial Award, naming him one of the most influential graduates in its history. Larry serves on the Board of Trustees for Azusa Pacific University.

Larry and Dr. Deb Walkemeyer have been married since 1978 and they write and speak frequently on marriage. They have two adult daughters. Larry enjoys snow skiing, waterskiing, biking, mission trips, and long walks on the beach.